HORIZON

NOVEMBER, 1960 · VOLUME III, NUMBER 2

HORIZON
A Magazine of the Arts

NOVEMBER, 1960 · VOLUME III, NUMBER 2

PUBLISHER
James Parton

EDITOR
Joseph J. Thorndike, Jr.
MANAGING EDITOR
William Harlan Hale
ASSOCIATE EDITORS
Ralph Backlund
Robert Emmett Ginna
ASSISTANT EDITORS
Ada Pesin
Jane Wilson
CONTRIBUTING EDITOR
Margery Darrell
EDITORIAL ASSISTANTS
Shirley Abbott, Caroline Backlund,
Alan Doré, Katherine Mayor
COPY EDITOR
Mary Ann Pfeiffer
Assistants: Rebecca R. Barocas, Ruth Limmer

ART DIRECTOR
Irwin Glusker
Assistant: Elton Robinson

ADVISORY BOARD
Gilbert Highet, *Chairman*
Frederick Burkhardt   Oliver Jensen
Marshall B. Davidson   Jotham Johnson
Richard M. Ketchum

EUROPEAN CONSULTING EDITOR
J. H. Plumb
Christ's College, Cambridge

EUROPEAN BUREAU
Gertrudis Feliu, *Chief*
28 Quai du Louvre, Paris

CIRCULATION DIRECTOR
Richard V. Benson

HORIZON is published every two months by
American Horizon, Inc., a subsidiary of American
Heritage Publishing Co., Inc., 551 Fifth Avenue,
New York 17, N. Y.
Single Copies: $3.95
Annual Subscriptions: $18.00 in the U.S. & Can.
$19.00 elsewhere

Second-Class postage paid at New York, N.Y.

HORIZON welcomes contributions but can assume
no responsibility for such unsolicited material.

COVER: When Benozzo Gozzoli painted this rapt little band of angels in 1459, he unhesitatingly gave them softly undulant robes, splendid wings, and the further support of rainbow clouds. Not that he had ever seen an angel himself (how many mortals have?)—he was simply following a well-established convention. How that convention grew up is discussed in an article, on page 26, on the iconography of heavenly beings. Gozzoli's angels may be seen in the chapel of the Palazzo Medici-Riccardi in Florence.

FRONTISPIECE: The Trojan horse, that eternal symbol of deceit, was an innocent-looking wooden effigy filled with armed and waiting Greeks. When the Milanese painter Giuseppe Arcimboldo addressed himself to this idea, he carried it a step further: omitting the wood, he composed his horse entirely of the writhing bodies of soldiers. Its eyes are two dark heads, its mane a row of flaming torches. Arcimboldo's grotesqueries were much admired by the Hapsburgs, who made him court painter at Prague from 1562 to 1587. Today he is admired by the surrealists, who look on him as a precursor.

THE ARTFUL BANKER

David Rockefeller's buying program

makes the Chase Manhattan Bank

the greatest corporate patron of art

Among the works of art bought for the new skyscraper, bottom left, are: top tier, a 19th-century hunting scene and a 1910 still life; next, a head by Leon Golub and a Fritz Glarner non-objective tondo; below, Robert Goodnough's The Survivors. *Opposite, David Rockefeller sits in front of José Guerrero's* Fire and Apparitions.

The officers and employees of the Chase Manhattan Bank are now moving into their new head office building, a sixty-story shaft designed by Skidmore, Owings and Merrill to glisten above the financial district in downtown Manhattan. Forsaken, as they move, are the graceful roll-top desks, the walnut paneling, and the grimy gingerbread of their former quarters in the same block; before them only smooth surfaces, cool light walls, Mies van der Rohe chairs, and severely simple functionalism.

All about them in their shiny new home hang vast, vivid canvases—many of them relentlessly avant-garde—in the lobbies and along the concourse on the ground floor, in the executive dining rooms and in the cafeteria, in the lounges and in the reception areas, in the conference rooms and in the clerical bull pens. Smaller paintings or other art objects decorate the private offices of the executives, floor upon floor, all the way from the third to the eighteenth. Before long, moreover, abstract sculptures will sprout up in the plaza outside the new building. The bank's budget for all these goodies is $510,700.

The Chase Manhattan's art program blazes no new trail. Scores of corporations have been investing heavily in contemporary art, much of it abstract. But the Chase Manhattan purchases dwarf all the others, at least financially. The bank's officers plan to organize a continuing series of exhibitions; new paintings will be regularly acquired; gifts will go from the permanent collection to museums. The guiding spirit of the program is the vice-chairman of the Chase Manhattan Board, David Rockefeller.

Whence this patronage of the controversial by staid, prudent bankers? Is it not daring—even rash? Not really. It is good business, as the officers of another bank, the Manufacturers Trust, were pleased to learn. In 1954 they moved their Fifth Avenue branch across the street into new quarters hung with modern paintings, including a Klee and a Miró; in the first year the number of accounts opened went up 31 per cent and the profits went up 200 per cent. Figures like these make a banker think.

As Jean Cocteau observed tartly not long ago, *"Le conformisme anticonformiste est à la mode. L'avant-garde est devenue le classicisme du vingtième siècle."*

Still, there are those in the world of business who harbor doubts. What, they may be led to wonder, would David's grandfather have thought of such goings-on? They may find an answer on the following pages.

An underworld report to John D. on the values of modern art

By PETER LYON

A summer afternoon in 1960. We are in Hell. To be more precise, we have a view of the afternoon sun sifting, pleasantly warm, through the maple trees and onto the veranda of the Chthonian Country Club, which is, of the many golf clubs in Hell, by far the most exclusive. It is, indeed, precisely the sort of country club where we should not be astonished to come upon the senior John D. Rockefeller, and, sure enough, here the old gentleman is, rocking back and forth in his rocking chair.

One should not assume that John D. is a permanent resident of Hell. Quite the contrary. He was, to be sure, consigned here by the historians who were his contemporaries, but theirs was by no means the final voice. In fact, he is a solid tithe-paying resident of the Baptist Heaven and can be counted upon to lift his voice in the celestial choir every Sunday morning.

The Hell of it is, he likes to play golf. And since there are no golf courses in Heaven (the game being, of course, one of the Devil's most aggravating torments), he must come here to play it. In consequence, he is here six days out of seven, and as often out of temper. Today, for example, his wretchedness derives from a slice in his drive that has sent his score for nine holes rocketing up past sixty. Has he been waggling too much on the backswing? Has he been lifting his head? It is hard to say. Perhaps one, perhaps the other. And just now, when he needs to bring his full power of concentration to bear on the question, there has come disquieting news about his youngest grandson, David. Fretfully he reaches forward and touches a bell on the table beside him.

Instantly there appears before him a fiend, who bows and rolls his eyes wickedly.

FIEND. What'll it be, Pop?

JOHN D. I have a job for you.

FIEND. Shoot.

JOHN D. I have just heard that the officers of the Chase Manhattan Bank are spending $510,700 on art, presumably to decorate their new head office building in Manhattan.

FIEND. So what? You a Philistine, or something?

JOHN D. The last time one of my family got mixed up with art in public, he hired a man named Diego Rivera to paint a mural in Rockefeller Center. Rivera stuck a picture of Lenin right in the middle of it. In *our* Center! Of course, it had to be destroyed.

FIEND. Naturally. [*He clucks his tongue.*]

JOHN D. And now here is my grandson David, allegedly putting up more art. He's vice-chairman of the Chase Manhattan Board of Directors, you know. But what on earth's got into him? A banker spending five hundred and ten thousand, seven hundred dollars on art! What next?

FIEND. [*sympathetically*] Beats the hell out of me!

JOHN D. I want you to find out if it's true. Sounds crazy to me, but maybe they're actually doing it. If so, I want you to find out all about it—whose idea it is, what kind of art they're buying, and why, and what people think about it. I want facts and figures.

There is time only for the light to fade into darkness and then to brighten again before we see that the old gentleman is once more restively rocking in the same chair, and lo! here, all at once, the fiend reappears. He sits down next to Rockefeller and massages his cloven hoofs, breathing hard.

FIEND. Jeekers! All over the Metropolitan, all over the Whitney, all over the Museum of Modern Art, around and down and around the Guggenheim, back and forth in the Stable and the Betty Parsons—

JOHN D. The stable? Where have you been? Out at some race track?

FIEND. [*loftily*] The Stable and the Betty Parsons just happen to be very recherché art galleries. Very In. Very U. Anyway, I'm pooped.

JOHN D. [*gruffly*] I don't suppose you found time to see my grandson David?

FIEND. Charming! Affable, friendly, couldn't be nicer.

JOHN D. [*Nods, pleased.*] Always fond of the boy. [*more crisply*] Well? How about this art nonsense? Not true, eh?

One of the largest canvases purchased by the Chase Manhattan Bank is Evening Images *(60″ x 72″), painted in 1958 by Kyle Morris, one of the New York group of abstract expressionists.*

FIEND. True? Of course it's true. What's more, they're all as excited about it as Teller with his H-bomb. Why not? Everybody's talking about it.

JOHN D. [*dryly*] I daresay they are.

FIEND. Here's a clipping from *Forbes*, the financial magazine, congratulating Chase Manhattan. Quote. They are helping to prove that business and artistic expression are not mutually antipathetic. Unquote.

JOHN D. [*heavily*] So it's true, is it?

FIEND. Wait a minute, will you? Wait a minute! Clippings from all over! From *Reader's Digest*! From *Fortune*! Why, David says the publicity alone is worth—

JOHN D. [*scandalized*] Publicity!

FIEND. Certainly the publicity. Don't forget, Pop, these days Rockefellers go out of their *way* to get publicity.

JOHN D. [*Wags his head.*] Oh, yes—yes, of course.

FIEND. Anyway, David says the publicity alone has already repaid the five hundred thousand they're spending.

JOHN D. [*fussily*] The sum is five hundred and *ten* thousand, seven hundred.

FIEND. It'll be more than that, before they're through. What do they care? It's all deductible. Legitimate business expense.

JOHN D. [*struck*] That's so, isn't it?

FIEND. Yip. Times have changed, Pop. And you should see that bank's new head office building! Sixty floors shooting straight up out of the ground. Looks like a great big shiny new brick of ice cream. And inside! Of course, it hadn't been finished when I was there, but you could see what it would be like. All cool and clean and bare . . .

JOHN D. [*Sniffs.*] Sounds like a hospital.

FIEND. It *is* a little antiseptic. That's how come the art.

JOHN D. But half a million dollars' worth?

FIEND. You don't seem to understand. They've got a lot of wall space, including private offices for one hundred and sixteen vice-presidents! This thing has got scope—you've got to envision it. The way they're buying art, they've practically got a lock on the market. Can you grasp what that means?

JOHN D. Just barely. [*He gets up and commences to prowl thoughtfully to and fro.*] I see what happened, now. You say each of one hundred and sixteen vice-presidents gets to

The Chase Manhattan Bank's untitled collage by Conrad Marca-Relli is built up of cutout shapes made of unprimed canvas which the artist first glues down and then proceeds to paint.

have a painting in his private office? Poor David. Outvoted.

FIEND. [*Laughs.*]

JOHN D. You find it funny?

FIEND. Pop, it was mostly David's idea.

JOHN D. I do not believe it. I *will* not believe it.

FIEND. Though I must say the stories differ. [*He consults his notes.*] Some say it was David's idea, some say it was the architect's idea. Gordon Bunshaft—he's one of the architects —*he* says it was like the chicken and the egg. What *I* think is, *I* think they just decided to put a lot of modern paintings on their walls because everybody else is putting a lot of modern paintings on their walls. It's the thing to do, these days, if you're a big, blue-chip, American businessman and want to show how progressive you are.

JOHN D. What! *Progressive?*

FIEND. Oh, sure. Inland Steel, Heinz, Reynolds Metals, Seagram, Manufacturers Trust, International Business Machines, Standard Oil—

JOHN D. [*Clutches at his chair.*] Not Standard Oil!

FIEND. I'm telling you, art is big business, these days. Take

the Manufacturers Trust. They open a new branch on Fifth Avenue, buy a few pictures to hang on the wall, not worth much, maybe thirty or forty thousand dollars, and three years later, when they have them appraised, guess what?

JOHN D. [*hopefully*] Worthless?

FIEND. Up 300 per cent and more customers than ever before! [*John D. lowers himself into his chair, with a dazed expression.*] Kind of makes you think, doesn't it? Ever had an investment that went up 300 per cent in three years?

JOHN D. [*thoughtfully*] Once or twice. [*He rocks faster and faster.*] Smart boy, David. I always knew it. So quite a few bankers and businessmen are buying pictures, eh?

FIEND. It's the new game, and anybody can play.

JOHN D. Ha! But it takes a Rockefeller to lay down the rules of the game, right? [*He cackles.*] First rule is to grab off the best paintings. [*sharply*] Who's picking David's paintings for him?

FIEND. A committee of connoisseurs unparalleled on the entire planet. Alfred H. Barr and Dorothy Miller of the Museum of Modern Art, Robert Beverly Hale of the Metro-

Carburetor *by Walter Murch is the work of an artist well known for still lifes that are in sharp contrast to the abstract style.*

politan Museum, James Johnson Sweeney, lately of the Guggenheim Museum, Perry Rathbone of the Boston Museum of Fine Arts, and the aforesaid Gordon Bunshaft.

JOHN D. [*with quiet satisfaction*] That's my grandson.

FIEND. [*blandly*] And when the paintings they choose have appreciated in value—say, when a picture they've bought for $2,000 is appraised at $4,000—David has got it all figured out that he'll give it to some deserving museum, declare a capital gain, and use the $2,000 profit to buy another painting to take the place of the first one. Neat?

JOHN D. Um. [*after a thoughtful pause*] What if the paintings *de*preciate?

FIEND. How can they, when they've been selected by such an august committee, the members of which are sought after more and more to advise on still other purchases, by still other collectors?

JOHN D. So that's the way it works. [*He nods appreciatively.*] Not bad. Lot of other buyers, are there, to keep the prices up?

FIEND. Thousands of 'em. It's the latest fashion. Instead of

an extra mink coat or a winter in Miami Beach, now you buy the latest paintings and get invited to all the posh openings.

JOHN D. Good. Good. [*He rocks contentedly.*] Not that it matters, I suppose, but . . . you've seen the paintings they're buying, of course? [*The fiend's eyes commence to glow like hot coals.*] I was wondering—what are they like?

FIEND. Well . . . [*He grins behind his hand.*]

JOHN D. [*apprehensively*] What's the matter?

FIEND. [*straight-faced again*] It's not so easy to describe them. They're oil paintings, on canvas, and—

JOHN D. [*sarcastically*] I didn't expect they'd be old clothes tacked up on boards.

FIEND. [*Nods.*] I've seen a few of those, too . . .

JOHN D. *What?*

FIEND. . . . but in the Chase Manhattan collection? No. At least, not yet. But most of the Chase Manhattan purchases are certainly controversial.

JOHN D. [*aghast*] Controversial! You mean they're more political propaganda?

In Late Day (Homage to the Square) is a recent work of German-born Josef Albers, influential teacher at the Bauhaus and later at Black Mountain College and Yale.

FIEND. [*judiciously*] No-o-o, not what you'd call political, exactly. Although there's one critic—let's see now. [*He shuffles through his notes.*] Here we are—the critic for *The New Republic*. He says they are, quote, a splendid artistic equivalent of Eisenhower Republicanism in politics. Unquote.

JOHN D. [*puzzled*] That doesn't sound very political. [*exasperated*] What do you mean, David's pictures are controversial? I ask you this one simple thing: describe them. What are they pictures *of*? Why do you torment me?

FIEND. [*Grins.*] All part of our infernally expert service, Pop. I tell you what I'll do: I'll let you see for yourself. [*He dives into his dispatch case and emerges with a handful of photographs.*] Here.

JOHN D. Ah. [*He inspects the pictures with growing bewilderment.*] What *are* these?

FIEND. Pictures of paintings by abstract expressionists, also sometimes known as action painters, also referred to as the New York School.

JOHN D. And you mean to tell me David is buying these? Or is this just another of your tiresome, hellish jokes?

FIEND. If it is, the best part of the joke is that these paintings look great on the walls of the new bank building. [*John D. shoots him a suspicious look.*] That's a fact. They look great. Why not? What's wrong with a big splash of color on a big blank wall?

JOHN D. But are these really paintings?

FIEND. Real hand-painted oil paintings, all Art and yards wide.

JOHN D. But there were *other* kinds of paintings. I'm *sure* there were. I remember them.

FIEND. They're still around. But they're not new, so nobody pays much attention to them.

JOHN D. So this is mostly what David is buying?

FIEND. Yip.

JOHN D. Can't he buy a few of the other kinds of paintings?

FIEND. Sure. He has to. Remember his one hundred and sixteen vice-presidents? Each of them has his own office. Each office is decorated to fit his personal taste. Each vice-president gets to pick his own desk (from five models), his own chair (from four models), the chairs for his visitors, the drapes for his window (or windows, if he's a senior vice-president), and the rug for his floor.

10

Elmer Bischoff, painter of Cityscape with Orange Light, *is one of the group of San Francisco artists who formerly worked in the abstract style but are now turning to landscape and the human figure.*

JOHN D. [*mildly*] My, haven't times changed!

FIEND. And he also gets to pick a painting to hang on his wall. Within, of course, a certain price range. Now every one of these one hundred and sixteen vice-presidents knows very well that David is hipped on this abstract expressionist art.

JOHN D. [*Winces.*] Don't!

FIEND. So wouldn't you think they'd all belly up and clamor to have an abstract expressionist painting to hang on their wall? [*He wags his head.*] You know how many of the one hundred and sixteen have picked an abstract painting? [*John D., fascinated, has stopped rocking completely.*] There may be more now, but when I was there the number was four. Four, out of one hundred and sixteen.

JOHN D. [*elated*] Why, that's just wonderf— [*Then a new thought strikes him; he stops dead and assumes a fierce frown.*] But that's disgraceful! Very disloyal of them, when the vice-chairman of their board of directors has clearly indicated that he's trying to remold the whole public image of bankers and banking! Well? Does that complete your report?

FIEND. Unless you have some questions.

JOHN D. I see two possible conclusions. [*He studies the pic-tures dubiously.*] On the one hand, these paintings are a new and wonderful development in the world of art, and David is in on something pretty exciting. [*He holds a picture out at arm's length to study it.*] Well? That's a possibility, isn't it?

FIEND. You've got that picture upside down.

JOHN D. [*angrily*] The only other conclusion is that your report is a nonsensical string of lies and poppycock, and that you are impudent enough to try to palm off on me these daubs as the sort of thing my David would pay good money for! [*He waggles an indignant forefinger at the fiend.*] Now then, for once tell me the truth—which of these conclusions is the right one?

FIEND. That's the Hell of it, Pop. You'll never find out here.

JOHN D. [*with dignity*] I see. [*He rises.*] I might have known. Well—I don't want you to think me ungrateful. Here. This is for all the trouble you've gone to. [*He hands the fiend a shiny new dime.*]

Peter Lyon, a free-lance writer and frequent contributor to HORIZON, *wrote "The Adventurous Angels" for May, 1959.*

Poised above the Rhine in Düsseldorf is one of the most elegant little skyscrapers in the world: the slender 24-story

THE NEWEST INVASION OF EUROPE

By REYNER BANHAM

Of the American-born skyscrapers now erupting in numbers above centuries-old townscapes, some are brilliant but all remain challenging strangers in the land

Mannesmann shaft (1958). With its nighttime glow it recalls its much larger American prototype, New York's Seagram building

Queen Victoria does not feature largely in the architectural history of the age to which she gave her name, yet at one point legend credits her with an action that was decisive in the architectural history of London. On the corner of the almost unspoiled eighteenth-century street in which I work stands the graceless brown brick pile of Queen Anne's Mansions, built almost ninety years ago. Standing fourteen stories tall in its sparse Gothic detailing, it was London's first high building—and for eighty years its last, since its erection was followed by a wave of almost penal legislation that made profitable construction of tall buildings impossible. Officially, that legislation was concerned with the heights that fire appliances could reach and with other matters of public concern, but legend insists that the real motive behind the laws was that Queen Victoria, discovering that the unlovely backside of the Mansions was visible from her palaces across St. James's Park, let it be known to her faithful ministers that —once more—she was not amused.

Whatever the truth of the story, the result of the legislation is plain to see. London, which early rivaled New York in the race for the clouds, got stopped off at about 100 feet, above which no habitable room or usable office could be built. A few noncommercial towers penetrated the 100-foot ceiling in the 1920's—notably those designed by Charles Holden for the old London Passenger Transport Board and for London University—and a few were proposed out of

commercial bravado by tycoons like Gordon Selfridge, who wanted one on top of his department store in Oxford Street. But London as a whole leveled off at seven or eight stories.

Something similar seems to have happened in most other sizable European cities. Even without special legislation, such as that accompanying Baron Haussmann's remaking of Paris, there is a strong tradition of control over building in every anciently chartered or incorporated city on the Continent; and the fear of fire (or other social pressures) plus a degree of aesthetic displeasure led to height restrictions similar to those in London.

Today, however, London and most other European capitals (and some noncapitals) have tall buildings either projected or completed. Not very tall by American standards —we call them "pocket" skyscrapers—they are still tall enough to rise boldly above the fairly uniform skyline of the European metropolis.

Between the buildings of the nineteenth century and the new pocket skyscrapers, there is a great gulf. It is a mental and cultural gulf concerned, quite simply, with the idea of a skyscraper. The fact that the leveling off of European cities at five to eight stories gives many of them a higher *average* building height than Manhattan Island is surprising but not significant. Who cares about averages? A statistic must always give way before such emotional truths as that one *very* tall building is worth a whole town of middling ones—as

TEXT CONTINUED ON PAGE 16

13

INGE GOERTZ-BAUER

Architects' Journal

HENK SNOEK

Left: Düsseldorf's newest skyscraper, the Phoe-nix-Rheinrohr building, consists of three very thin slabs. The mid-portion where they overlap is a core of elevators and other services, with the result that the building, unlike the bulkier American ones, has no windowless interior offices. Above: Looming above London's uniformly low skyline are a few crisp new buildings. Eastbourne Terrace (top) has two towers, the taller of which is shown here, and is considered London's best skyscraper development. Castrol House (bottom) looks especially fine at night with its green glass spandrels lit from within.

Milan's skyscrapers include Western Europe's tallest so far, the 33-story Pirelli building (right), and one of its most unusual, the bizarre Torre Velasca (below). By night or day, the Pirelli building is the epitome of contemporary Italian taste. A version of the so-called "lenticular" plan, it incorporates the elevators in the thick part of the "lentil" and the utility stacks in its pointed ends. While the Torre Velasca is completely modern inside, its exterior has the rude, graceless strength of a medieval defense tower—from which, in part, its architect Ernesto Rogers drew inspiration.

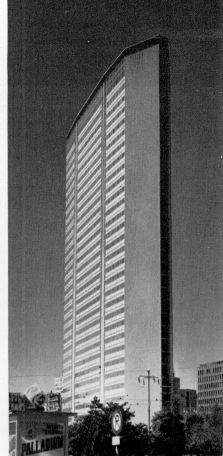

PHOTOGRAPHS PUBLIFOTO

TEXT CONTINUED FROM PAGE 13

witness the undying fascination of the Eiffel Tower. After Gustave Eiffel's masterpiece, no very tall towers were built in Europe, whereas the United States, and New York in particular, went on building higher and higher as the old century expired and the twentieth began.

By the turn of the century, the visual image of skyscraper New York was familiar to Europeans through magazine illustrations and literary descriptions; the latter, being the work of men of "literary culture," were usually hostile to the whole skyscraper concept. But around 1910 the rebel bands of cultural roughnecks, such as the cubists and futurists, began to welcome the skyscraper and set it up as the mental symbol of their new Utopia, the mechanized metropolis that could not exist in Europe without the destruction of the old metropolises or the creation of new ones on virgin sites. It became, for Walter Gropius, "the crystal symbol" of a new, clean world in which the immemorial shames and squalors of feudal, imperial Europe would be sloughed off forever.

The first of these Utopian dream cities was the futurists' Milano 2000, a dynamic metropolis of *grattacieli*; it was followed by Auguste Perret's *villes-tours* immediately after World War I and Le Corbusier's Ville Contemporaine of 1922, with its clustered *gratte-ciels*. Meanwhile the Friedrichstrasse and Chicago *Tribune* Tower competitions encouraged German modernists to hope that their dream of a heroic *Wolkenkratzer* might be realized. It wasn't, but many of their projects finished up in a special issue of the Dutch magazine *Wendingen*, together with a project by the editor, Theo van de Wijdeveld, to replan Amsterdam with a double file of twenty-story towers down the axis of the Vondel Park.

But a dream it remained throughout the twenties and the thirties. Much solid thinking, as well as emotional capital, was invested in the dream—Le Corbusier, for instance, has probably devoted more sweat and imagination to the design of tall buildings than any man living, with the galling result that the first "European" skyscraper was built in Rio de Janeiro: the Ministry of Education building, though designed by a Brazilian team under Lucio Costa, was based on sketches by Le Corbusier and imbued with his ideas.

The realization of this dream on European ground is a phenomenon of the last ten years. Of course, it is not, in truth, a realization of the futurist dream, because it involves the building not of wholly new skyscraper cities but only of small skyscrapers in existing cities. This is what precipitates the "skyscraper situation" in Europe. The

building of a tall block in an American city is, one supposes, simply a practical solution to a practical need (even if it includes intangibles like corporate prestige), and it fulfills, one also supposes, an almost traditional American pattern of town making. But in Europe the creation of a tall tower is an exciting, antitraditional gesture, conducted in tradition-loaded surroundings. The work will not, therefore, be judged on its own isolable merits but as a piece of the town, and to a greater or lesser degree this is how all skyscrapers are judged in Europe. A similar situation may not be so far away in America. Quite apart from the purely mechanical problems of congestion, the characteristic urban silhouette of certain United States cities is being recognized as something valuable in itself, and it begins to be possible to ask whether the blunt, flat-topped profile of the Chase Manhattan building (see "The Artful Banker," page 4—ED.) will not spoil the skyline of lower Manhattan. Again, at a closer range, there is a growing appreciation of the part played by the nonskyscrapers on Park Avenue, and alarm that Lever House and the Seagram building (widely regarded as the last two stages in the perfection of an ideal glass-box building) may suffer, aesthetically, from the less well-designed towers on their flanks.

In Europe, worries of this kind *precede* the erection of the buildings, for skyscrapers are still restricted to a few cities. Paris, with L'Opération Maine-Montparnasse and the Immeuble Croulebarbe still in the project stage, as yet has no structures of skyscraper form and bulk. Nor has Amsterdam, in spite of Wijdeveld's plans. Brussels has just acquired the Centre Rogier, which is no masterpiece; Rome has none; Copenhagen has Arne Jacobsen's elegant SAS building, a "Son of Seagram." West Berlin lacks the spectacular skymark of democratic capitalism that the political situation would seem to require; neither the Berlin Hilton hotel nor the Telefunken Haus der Elektrizität is really up to the job, in spite of the technical excellencies that both exhibit.

Discussion of European skyscrapers, their problems and prospects, must be for the present a discussion of buildings in Düsseldorf, London, and Milan, partly because of architectural quality, partly because of all the thinking and talking that have gone into their design and siting. Düsseldorf gets into the big league on the strength of two buildings of considerable interest that introduce the European skyscraper problem without entanglement in its knottier involutions.

As townscape, Düsseldorf is

CENTRAL PRESS

London officials, who have greater control over their cityscapes, recently rejected on aesthetic grounds this proposed office building on Piccadilly Circus.

CONTINUED ON PAGE 124

By HUGH MacLENNAN

THE ROUT
of the
CLASSICAL
TRADITION

The reasons for throwing the classics out of

education—though sound enough at the time—

no longer obtain today, and so the young are

beginning to set up the cry: "We are cheated!"

Just after New Year's in 1960 I was asked to read a paper on the subject of the classics in education. I was astonished. Truly I believed I had sat through the deathwatch on the classics twenty-five years ago; had listened to the symptoms of a once-great personality expiring from malnutrition, contempt, and disappointment. I was aware that what is called "the Latin requirement" still lingers in a few curricula, but this survival had seemed no more significant than the retention of the little residual piece of steel, still called a bayonet, on the end of a rifle of a soldier in an atomic army. When somebody remarked that only a third of today's college presidents can translate the texts of the degrees they hand out at convocations, I had believed the figure exaggerated. I once taught Latin and Greek myself. But the subject began to fascinate me; chiefly, I suppose, because somebody was still around who remembered the classics and wondered whether more had been lost than gained when they were allowed to perish from the system. Although I work with the young three days a week, like them and admire them, I have tried to avoid thinking about theories of education these many years. In my time there have been as many of them as there have been theories of economics, and the successful ones, by which I mean the ones which were adopted, all tend in the same general direction: they conform to the producer-consumer cycle. But lately we have been hearing a peculiar whirring sound emerging from the young people, and quite recently it has been articulate in three terrible words that should make older people tremble: "We are cheated!" The young not only understand, they are beginning to say openly that what has cheated them more efficiently than anything else has been the educational system they are offered. The best of them transcend it as the best transcend almost anything, but the best also say that the average student today is graduated naked to his enemies.

Dante Alighieri

There is a vacuum in the system and the young know it, and there are probably millions of older people who know it, too. It occurs to me, perhaps wrongly, that this vacuum began to appear when the classical tradition began to die out. So I brought myself—and "brought myself" are the *mots justes*—to think back a little on what has happened. Though I do not care much for Aristotle's personality and know that the scientists abhor his favorite question, I have never found it profitable to dodge that question very long. It is: "What is the purpose?" So what is the purpose, the over-all purpose, of the educational system that almost every articulate young person today believes is cheating him?

On the university level in North America the casual observer takes it for granted that the chief purpose of the system is the teaching of a variety of skills, many of which have no direct connection with one another. The faculties with the highest prestige are the skill-teaching ones: medicine, engineering, commerce, law, dentistry, and—in some more comprehensive institutions—farming, hotelkeeping, and the like, together with as many contingent schools and institutions as the establishment can support, or be persuaded to support. Oddly enough, most first-rate universities still proclaim that the Faculty of Arts and Sciences is their core, and that the Faculty of Graduate Studies and Research is their finest flower. Lip service to the arts is paid in proportion to the degree of neglect from which they suffer, but the fact remains that on this side of the ocean the majority of students registered in arts courses are girls.

Therefore, I think it no exaggeration to say that since the war the universities have been half-educating a substantial number of girls, and have been training, at least in terms of the respective assignments, a somewhat larger number of boys to qualify for the higher income brackets. Science is encouraged because it is essential to most of the skill-teaching courses, but for one genuine scientist in each student body there must be thirty who take the courses only because they are required as preliminaries to whatever skill-teaching faculty they are registered in. Science, it is admitted, is still regarded as essential. But arts are not. An increasing number of students, doubtless repeating what they have heard from their parents, are now uttering new versions of the old question the Latin teachers used to await with the sensations of a man in a dentist's chair anticipating the moment when the dentist would reach for the drill: "Sir, what is the *use* of English?" "Sir, what is the *use* of French unless you live in the Province of Quebec?" "Sir, what is the *use* of history and philosophy?"

The students, it would seem, are more honest than the educational officials. They are certainly franker than the American engineering dean who stated that the ideal of his faculty was to produce a broadly educated man, and then, in the same speech, proceeded to boast that the reason why more students were enrolled in his faculty than in any other was because engineers in that particular year were enjoying the highest per capita income of any professional group in the country.

No doubt of it, the school authorities have at last persuaded the public to spend more money on education than the public has ever spent on it before, or to be more precise, to turn over more money for the educational authorities to spend as they see fit. The continent has blossomed with shiny new high schools homogenized out of glass, brick, and plastics, full of light and air and concert halls, and these are improvements on the grim old structures that often were mistaken for the town jail. But so far as the instruction is concerned, I don't see how anyone can argue (at least not without laughing) that the principal purpose of the modern grade school is to turn out educated youths. Perhaps its purpose is more humane. Education is not a thing designed for comfort, but for survival and for the development of a personality our ancestors believed was valuable in itself, and, moreover (their evidence may have been inadequate), valuable to the God who counted every hair on the personality's head. Perhaps it is cruel—certainly many psychiatrists thought it was, at least for a while—to encourage individualism in a world like ours or, for that matter, in any world. Adjustment is the word. So it would seem that the over-all purpose of most primary education in modern America is to turn out friendly people free of neuroses and the critical sense that makes its possessor gnash his teeth at the calculated insults to the human intelligence perpetrated by politicians and advertisers in a television-consumer society.

Anyway, this is the general picture in the schools, and I believe its modern perfection required the total elimination of the classical tradition, which first was attacked by the educational revolution of the mid-nineteenth century. This revolution, however, had some results which its instigators, most of whom were honorable men, did not foresee.

From the moment education came under the control of the state, two developments were certain to follow. Education would enter the area of democratic politics; the educational system sooner or later would betray the usual symptoms of a bureaucracy. In the nineteenth century this seemed less dangerous than it does now, because then democracy was more of a living reality. Its issues were competently debated in small towns and on the hustings. Politics had not yet become a branch of the advertising business.

It has now, with the results that political success depends more on popularity than on ability and that the easiest way to become popular is to take the road of least resistance. Applied to education, this has meant that the officials in the system who were ambitious to rise were generally the ones who told the public what the public wanted to hear. By modern methods (remember the propaganda of two decades ago?) boys and girls could become educated without having to work. The play-method would teach them all the grammar and arithmetic they were required to know; democratic citizenship habits would be acquired in the schools—as indeed they were, if we understand them to mean what they do now; the teacher would teach better if he or she were careful to be popular with the class; discipline must be relaxed so that no neuroses could develop; standards must be lowered lest a stupid child acquire the inferiority feelings that breed neuroses. By now the story is so familiar it needs no repeating; we are left with the results of it. And the educators who introduced this system have created a pattern in which education, instead of leading society, follows a blindfolded society, wearing a double blindfold of its own.

Meanwhile, within the workings of the system the bureaucracy burgeoned. In the past, the teacher and the administrator were one and the same man. The college provost gave lectures and tutorials, the headmaster taught in the upper forms, administration was reduced to bare essentials. This seldom happens any more in a school or college because the chiefs are too busy to teach and, in many cases, even to see students except on convocation platforms. On the school level, we see the teacher, better paid than formerly but without prestige, coping with the age-old job of teaching the young. But he does so in a system in which he has no authority, in which his wishes and experience are little more considered than those of a private soldier in the army. Above him we see the successful "educator," who is usually a teacher graduated to the administrator's desk, a man somewhat privileged; and in his office he is an executive giving directives to teachers he barely knows, a businessman dealing with boards of external businessmen on more or less equal terms of prestige. But whether he likes it or not, these outside boards are his final courts of appeal. It is they on whom he depends for his success, his advancement, indeed his professional existence. People being as they are, he is generally compelled to deal with them on their terms and not on his own, and their terms are miles apart from those of the teachers who do the actual work in the schools and colleges.

In the days when the classical tradition reigned, there was nothing like this. The purpose of education was simple then, and the schools and colleges were so systemless that to the modern executive mind anything like them would be intolerable. Not only were there no IBM machines, there were not even typewriters. The purpose of education was merely to teach the student to read, to write, to learn basic mathematics, to work in a disciplined way, and finally to expose him, while doing this, to the best minds in civilization and to let the  classics become a part of him and at the same time to let the clarity of mathematics enter into his thinking.

The over-all purpose of education in those days was precisely as Bacon described it: "Studies serve for delight, for ornament, and for ability. Their chief use for delight is in privateness and retiring; for ornament, is in discourse; and for ability, is in the *judgment and disposition of affairs*." If I emphasize the last statement, it is only to remind the reader that in the days when our civilization was growing, judgment was valued more highly than any particular skill, and the ideal man of affairs was not a specialized executive but Aristotle's *phronimos*, the prudent, experienced man of goodwill with a wide perspective of men and events.

Bacon goes on: "For expert men can execute, and perhaps judge of particulars, one by one; but the general counsels, and the plots and marshalling of affairs, come best from those that are learned."

And again, because it was the essence of the classical insight that life is a fleeting thing and a rare privilege, that life must be lived: "To spend too much time in studies is sloth; to use them too much for ornament is affectation; to make judgment wholly by their rules is the humour of a scholar. They perfect nature, and are perfected by experience: for natural abilities are like natural plants that need pruning by study; and studies themselves do give forth directions too much at large, except they be bounded in by experience. Crafty men contemn studies; simple men admire them; and wise men use them: for they teach not their own use; but that is a wisdom without them and above them, won by observation."

Here, with unparalleled clarity, is contained the entire philosophy behind the old classical education. As for the technique and curriculum, Bacon is equally specific: "Reading maketh a full man, conference a ready man, and writing an exact man. Histories make men wise; poems, witty;

Isaac Newton

the mathematics, subtle; natural philosophy, deep; moral, grave; logic and rhetoric, able to contend." And he concludes this famous passage with the Ovidian line my old school used for its motto: *Abeunt studia in mores.* Hence it appears that the purpose of the old education was to produce a certain kind of man.

What manner of man he was, how remarkable was his variety within a coherent system of knowledge and values, the history of European, and especially of British and French, society shows very clearly.

He must not be judged—God forbid—by the German and American pedants of the Ph.D. mills which developed in the decadence of the tradition and aided its enemies in extinguishing it. During the Renaissance, he was the "new man" of his epoch, and he led the people of Europe out of a priest-ridden medievalism into the light of knowledge and discovery. Indeed, the chief word associated with the Renaissance is illumination; not comprehension, not the deep and precise understanding of particulars which comes from science, but illumination of thought, life, and society expressing itself in language, literature, music, architecture, art, life values, and —this above all—action.

In the modern connotation, a man trained in the classical tradition is obviously an amateur, and as such he is judged inadequate. He cannot fill a tooth, perform an abdominal, fire a rocket to the moon; he is relatively useless to the specific producer-consumer-repairer tasks which now have be-

come nearly the whole content of life. But when we look at his record in the past, we must admit that the classical tradition did quite a lot for civilization.

It enabled Dante and Petrarch, followed by the writers of every other nation of Europe, to mold the vernaculars by translating into them the light, knowledge, and methods of the mother cultures which had died. The classics underlay the literature and thought of the West as surely as Roman law underlies the Code Napoléon. In England they nourished nearly every genius of which the nation is proud. The classical ideal of clarity, applied to the clumsy and confused prose of the seventeenth century, enabled Dryden, Addison, Steele, Defoe, and Swift to forge the peerless linguistic instrument which made England's eighteenth century the most lucid period since the Age of Pericles. Inheriting a language purged of obscurities, Jefferson was able to write a Declaration of Independence so clear that ordinary men could understand it without a lawyer's help. No complex system produced these results. They came from hard-working teachers who stood no nonsense, who taught mathematics and languages, and who knew that clarity would come as a matter of course to anyone capable of becoming educated.

For how could a man be unclear if he had mastered a language in which it is impossible to be ambiguous without being ungrammatical, and if he had applied the Latin tenets of clarity to his own speech? Nor was this all: people classically trained had acquired a sort of human geometry which now has been lost. They understood the past not in detail but in its broad outlines; they knew that certain actions are bound to produce similar effects no matter where or when they are performed. The eighteenth-century gentleman may have been callous to the sufferings of the poor, indifferent to the cruelty of the laws. But he was tender to civilization itself, which he knew had come not from the masses but from a very small number of gifted individuals. It is impossible to imagine a statesman of Pitt's time dropping an atomic bomb, if he had one, on a city of an already defeated enemy. It is impossible to imagine him giving the orders to have one made. Above all, the classical tradition taught this: that the road of least resistance is sure to become the hardest road in the end, and that this road is usually followed by people whose minds are fragmented, who judge of particulars without relating them to the whole. Ruthless though the eighteenth-century politicians were, before the French Revolution they seldom deceived themselves.

If our statesmen today constantly deceive themselves, it is because they are too ignorant to understand where the road of least resistance leads. Most of them appear to know nothing of human geometry. Imagine, for instance, a modern revolutionary statesman addressing the people with the words of John Jay, first Chief Justice of the United States. Speaking only ten years after the Constitution had been drafted, it would have been easy for Jay to proclaim that a new era in humanity had dawned, that the old evils had been conquered by the glorious revolution, that mankind (pick any cliché you like) was now marching shoulder to shoulder into the broad uplands of prosperity, brotherhood, and justice for all. But what Jay actually did utter makes strange reading today: "I do not expect," he said, "that mankind will, before the millennium, be what they ought to be; and therefore, in my opinion, every political theory which does not regard them as being as they are, will prove abortive."

The classics can still teach this kind of human geometry to anyone who acquaints himself with them. Even when I was a boy there were vestiges of the tradition left in daily life. My father was one of them. He was a doctor who spent much of his earlier life in a very hard practice in a Cape Breton mining town, but thanks to his classical interests, he was not isolated there. He read Latin and Greek for pleasure; he read the philosophers. In retrospect I see him as one of the least provincially minded men I ever knew, even though he was full of Calvinist and Scotch quirks. He was democratic in his human dealings; not familiar, not a glad-hander, not a winner of friends and an influencer of people, but democratic enough, apparently, to make a hundred-odd workmen want to follow his hearse to a grave through a snow storm. I used to think him hidebound pretty often, and I also used to think him intolerant, for he was full of scorn for most of the things that were going on in the educational system, and he developed an increasing contempt for the mentality of politicians. I see now that although he entirely lacked modern social techniques, he was not often wrong. He objected to modern education because it failed to educate, and he objected to modern politicians not so much because they deceived the people as because they first deceived themselves. This self-deception he ascribed to the fuzziness and confusion of their language, which they used in an automatic manner that in time could do nothing else but cloud their thinking processes.

My father died just before World War II began, and he died knowing it was inevitable and why it was inevitable. This he understood not so much from reading the papers as from reading Thucydides. I have often wished he had lived a year and a half longer, for in 1940 he would have seen a classicist of genius rally the decent people of the world with no weapons but language well used and a vision of essentials as clear as a relief map. I know that Winston Churchill boasts that at Harrow he was a bad Latin scholar, but he was a product of the tradition. In his more reckless moments, he talks fustian, but never when the matter is important. Then his language is the sparest and most classical in measure of any writer in the last century. Churchill did not have to read Cicero and Demosthenes in the original to obtain his style; he got it by direct inheritance from Gibbon, Burke, and Chatham, who in turn got it from the primary sources.

It is gone now; to repeat, the classical tradition is gone so far beyond reasonable controversy that it makes no more sense to regret it than to regret the time when bankruptcy was considered a disaster and not a technique used by shrewd men to avoid their obligations. But we still want to live somehow or other, and so many people are beginning to think our survival depends on an improvement in the educational system that it may be worthwhile to examine why the classical tradition died. Nobody can think sensibly about today's educational needs unless he understands this, for the classics were attacked and defeated for reasons which do not obtain today.

It is commonly believed that the classics failed because they could not meet the competition of science. In a sense this is true, yet science was never hostile to a tradition which originated in the Greek skepticism whose greatest thinker inscribed over the doors of the first academy: "Let no man enter here who knows no geometry." Bacon and Newton wrote their scientific books in Latin; in our time scientists like Einstein and Oppenheimer were versed in the classics. No, it was not science that killed the tradition, for in a sense, science is a part of it, an outgrowth of its entire attitude. It was democracy which killed it— by insisting that education should abandon its role of illuminator of life in order to convert itself into a toolmaker for democracy's material needs and a healer of democracy's bodies. In this insistence I don't see how anyone can deny that democracy was entirely right.

Earl of Chatham

The primary needs of nineteenth-century democracy could not have been other than material, and at that period of history, it would have been criminal to have denied them the satisfaction they craved. Though adventurous minds were exhilarated by the prospect of exploring the new possibilities in science, the ordinary citizen's interest in science did not lie in the exploring of mysteries and the accumulation of knowledge. He wished to apply scientific aids to increase the wealth, to mitigate and finally abolish a poverty no longer unavoidable, to conquer what Mark Twain called "the ancient dominion of pain," to open as many new avenues of opportunity as possible. None of these aims could be satisfied by a tradition whose chief end was to produce a wise man with a sense of perspective and time. Around the middle of the last century, the classical tradition appeared to the avant-garde of educationists as a luxury which society could not afford, and by the end of the century it appeared a luxury to almost everybody. Many of its defenders were branded as coldhearted obscurantists, as some of them probably were. For what was the use of wisdom if it was only for a privileged few? What was the use of culture if the handful who possessed it were supported by the patience of a cultureless poor? Also there was greed—where was the profit in Latin and Greek? The greed of the business community on the one hand, the humanitarianism of the liberals on the other, insisting that poverty and disease must be conquered—these two mighty forces united in the nineteenth century to rout the classical tradition almost everywhere in North America.

But human society, as Montaigne says, "goes very incompetently about healing its ills." Humanitarians, like so many liberal revolutionaries, are apt to have extremely provincial minds. They are—Montaigne again—so impatient of what vexes them at any particular moment that they seek to get rid of it, reckless of the cost. They also like to succeed, and the path to a quick success is usually the path of least resistance. If you are an administrator or a politician, it is almost always that.

John Jay

Now I think the time has come when we can return to the basic question. Since a vacuum has been created in education by the death of the classical tradition, is it possible to discover anything with which the vacuum can be filled—as I, and many others, think it must be?

It is not possible, I should say, unless there is a large general understanding that the needs of modern democracy have changed out of recognition since men like Thomas Henry Huxley, Eliot of Harvard, and Sir William Dawson of McGill set out to satisfy the needs of a century ago. Their success is attested to by our present condition. Education has most certainly produced the toolmakers, the healers, the accountants, the distributors, the consumers; the totality of its success in doing this is now recognized on all levels. The old hostility of commerce to the academy has changed from a hostility toward something it considered snobbish and impractical to a vague feeling that too many professors are likely to harbor socialistic theories. Why commercial men should believe this, or worry about it if it is true, is a mystery to me, because if a modern nexus of corporations is not a collective under another name, I don't know what it is. But the old hostility is virtually gone now, and no wonder. Not

long ago at a debate conducted by the McGill Humanities Association, a representative of the Manufacturers' Association said that his body had come to the conclusion that higher education deserved all the support from business that it asked. According to him, consumer research efforts had turned up the interesting conclusion that college graduates are the best consumers we have.

Democracy in the last century was poor and partially in rags; its condition was similar to that of what we now call an "underdeveloped" country. But Western democracy is now so Croesus-rich that its most characteristic industry, advertising, must keep the producer-consumer wheel turning by constantly creating what it calls "new needs." Nineteenth-century democracy could not afford the humanities, as we have seen. But now the question is different. Now the question is: Can mid-twentieth-century democracy dare *not* to afford them? Its officials do not want them, do not admit they are valuable, and most of them know nothing important about them. But can they *dare*—and this is the right word—to tolerate much longer a system in which the humanities live the anemic existence of underprivileged beggars of the bad old days?

I would argue that they cannot, and for what seems to me a reason pretty hard to disregard. Specialized skills we now have in abundance, but hardly anyone in authority understands how to use them for any purpose save the production, distribution, and consumption of goods and services. On international levels we are floundering from one confusion to another, and we are getting scared. The West has reached the place where its leaders *want* to be able to fear Russia. The truth is that they, and we, are more afraid of ourselves. We are terrified inside by the galloping corruption produced by a now meaningless routine of production, distribution, and consumption. And this I know, because I teach the young.

When I said earlier that the young feel cheated, I meant just that, and from talking to dozens of them I know why, because they know why. When they read that the chief economic adviser of President Eisenhower says that the primary goal of the American government is "to maximize consumption," they feel those words in their nerve ends. They ask themselves: "Has life no more purpose than the dreary round of mating, raising families that will live as our parents do, working endlessly to make ends meet in a constantly more expensive society, unable really to enjoy ourselves, passing on the responsibility of doing something better to our children?" If the majority of young men avoid the humanities in the colleges, it is not because they are hostile to them. It is because their fathers urge them—indeed, the whole organized voice of modern society commands them—to install themselves in paying jobs at the earliest possible moment. Staring them in the face in the center of the treadmill is the Organization Man, and not one young person in a hundred likes him. How can he, when the Organization Man is unable to like himself?

So I believe that the revolution may now be nearing the point of full circle, and I think this because of the example of Russia.

No country on earth has been more firmly wedded to faith in material progress than the Soviet Union. Unlike ourselves, who do not let the right lobe of the brain know what the left lobe thinketh, the Soviets for years were unashamed materialists. Yet in recent years a new phenomenon has appeared in Russia: students, male as well as female, are being urged to enter the humanities, and at the moment no less than 55 per cent of them are engaged in these studies. Evidently the Russian leaders, more intelligent than the self-salesmen who have propelled themselves into the so-called "leadership" of the West, have concluded that a time has come when material requirements will be satisfied more or less automatically, and that there is now a need for the kind of education which will produce people capable of thinking in perspective. "The general counsels, and the plots and marshalling of affairs, come best from those that are learned"—quite possibly the present leaders of Russia go all the way with Bacon on that point. Doubtless the history taught in the Russian state-supported system is even more mythological than in ours. But if Russian students are now learning thoroughly at least one foreign language, if thousands of them are encouraged to study Latin, if 55 per cent of them are becoming acquainted with the old humanistic disciplines, then it is certain that within another generation Russia will be much more civilized than North America. As she will also be stronger in the materialistic sense, and have a better morale, it requires no feat of the imagination to see what this is going to mean for our descendants. They will (probably without conquest because conquest will be unnecessary) become a tired-out province in a world state dominated by Moscow.

So the question would seem to be more urgent than most of us think: Can anything be substituted for the classical tradition which is gone? Since men a century ago asked themselves what were the prime needs of democracy, and sought to satisfy them by building an education to satisfy them, we might do the same now. And it seems to me that our present needs can best be understood in terms of losses. What qualities, abilities, and attitudes have we lost as a result of the abandonment of the humanistic tradition?

The first loss, I should say, is the old belief that life is a coherent experience.

The second loss—the result of the first—is of the collective and individual self-confidence our forefathers knew, and which we ourselves knew for a brief while under Churchill's leadership in the last war.

The third loss—the result of the second—is the ancient respect for truth as something valuable and unassailable in itself, as something hard to find but precious, as something which cannot be juggled with by advertisers and politicians without regard to the final consequences, as something more important, however austere it may be, than conformity for the sake of comfort to any marketplace necessity of the moment.

The fourth loss—the result of the third—is the old belief that education cannot be easy, that it leads not to material security but to struggle, that at its best it is a pilgrim's progress to the heavenly city.

Therefore, I would say that education on all levels should get back to the primary business of education, which is to create an atmosphere in which these four losses will slowly be restored. In the long run, the most important question for a man or for a state is simply this: "What is the will of God?" I use this latter word with apology, and sometimes I think it should be retired from the language: it has been so debased that the people who use it seldom know what they mean. Use "Creator" instead if you like; use "the Life Force" or "the Prime Mover of Motions"; use "Nature," as long as you understand that nature in this sense is something more than the provider of static raw material for laboratory research. But what is truth? What is the purpose of life?

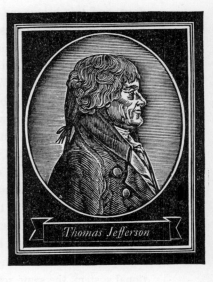

Thomas Jefferson

What is God's will? What matters here is not that these questions can never be adequately answered; what matters is that they must be *asked* if a society is to survive. And my reason for stating this categorically is based on experience and on nothing else; it rests solidly on the recorded experience of the human race.

In order to create an atmosphere in which questions like these again become important, some drastic steps will have to be taken, especially on primary levels in the system. On the one hand, the philosophy of "adjustment" will have to be thrown on the junk heap; on the other, the schools will have to stop smattering and seek to prepare students for the marriage of the two basic disciplines: theoretical science and the humanities properly studied. This marriage can never become an intimate one; at best it can be only the marriage of Rilke's two solitudes which protect and touch and greet each other.

If this general philosophy of education is accepted, the

next step is to stiffen the curriculum all the way down the line. I do not believe it is possible to restore the classics to the position they once occupied, although in a changed atmosphere I know that many more students would come forward to them than most people believe. But certainly the great books of our own and other languages, which are the classics' inheritors, can be used, as in some cases they are used even now.

But in order for them to be used properly, students must be taught to read, and by this I do not mean (in the phrase of Albert Jay Nock) merely passing printed matter through the mind. Nobody can read and understand a book unless he himself knows how to write after a fashion and to express himself on paper with reasonable clarity. Reading still maketh the full man and writing the exact one, and the reason why eighteenth-century people expressed themselves almost effortlessly was because they were trained to do so in the schools. They learned the use of their tools early in those days, and this brings me to another point in which it is a pleasure to call science itself to witness.

The neurologists have now proved that the old educational methods were better than ours for a reason beyond, apparently, any contradiction. When children are very young, their memories are excellent—better than they will ever be again —but their reasoning powers have not yet developed. This is not for psychological causes; it is for reasons purely physical, for reasons connected with the growth of the brain itself. By a method of trial and error, teachers in the past insisted on a vast amount of memory work in the lower grades. As a result, it was not difficult to produce a student aged fourteen who wrote passable Greek verse, who knew all his basic mathematics in his sleep, and at least one modern language.

If the cart had not been put before the horse in our educational system, the same results could be obtained now. With no hardship, a good student could reach high school in reasonable command of two other languages besides his own. He could know his grammar and spelling. He could know his basic mathematics up to the calculus. He could have at his disposal the tools which a developing reason could then employ. As only a small proportion of the human race seems capable of thinking rationally, not all of the pupils could proceed much further. But the vital elite could, and the rest would be no worse, and much better, for the knowledge they had acquired. If Russian students have mastered one language and the calculus at the equivalent of our tenth grade, and since few of our present college graduates have done either of these things, it would seem that the case against the present system has been pretty thoroughly laid.

I will now follow Sir Philip Sidney's example and come to you with a tale. It may not hold children from play or old men from the chimney corner, but if all of its implications are taken in, it may give you the interesting sensation of mice dancing up and down on your spine. It certainly gave me that feeling when it happened, and it still does whenever I remember it.

Shortly after the first election of Dwight D. Eisenhower to the presidency of the United States, I happened to be in Washington speaking at a luncheon held by the people who were backing the St. Lawrence Seaway bill in the Senate and House. After the speech was over, I realized that some of the audience had acquired the impression that I was a kind of trial balloon sent down unofficially to express the real views of the Canadian government on the matter. Nothing could have been further from the case; I was even more private a person than I am now. But I soon found myself at a table in the bar of the Statler Hotel surrounded by politicians and lobbyists who fired questions at me and who did not believe what I told them.

While the questioning was going on, I happened to look over my shoulder and see Dr. J. Robert Oppenheimer enter the room in company with another nuclear physicist. I guessed (correctly as it turned out when I had time to read the evening paper) that he was in Washington on atomic business, for he was, at that time, head of atomic research in the United States and the H-bomb was being built.

In order to change the subject, I said to the politicians, "I notice that a genius has come among us."

One of them glanced at Dr. Oppenheimer, did not recognize him, and when I told him the name, did not recognize that either.

"What does he do for a living?" he asked.

"For a living, I suppose he's still director of the Institute for Advanced Study in Princeton."

"A professor? Ugh."

I said that Dr. Oppenheimer was not a teaching professor, at least not principally, and that the Institute was no part of Princeton University. Then, assuming that everyone knew who Einstein was (he was still alive at the time), I added that the Institute was where Einstein had worked since his arrival in the United States.

The politician then looked at me, and with the sincerity of total innocence, he asked, "This Einstein, has he got anything real on the ball, or is it all theory?"

The politician, as I learned by looking up his record later in *Who's Who,* was a graduate of a middle-western American university.

Best known to Americans for his recent, highly praised novel The Watch that Ends the Night, *the Canadian Hugh MacLennan is also an essayist and professor of English literature at McGill University in Montreal. This essay is one of a new collection,* Scotchman's Return, *to be published by Charles Scribner's Sons this fall.*

Opposite: Winston Churchill as a fifteen-year-old schoolboy at Harrow

An Iconography of

HEAVENLY BEINGS

Why do angels have wings? In early Christian times God's messengers

walked as men. But after the sweeping conversions of the pagan world

Christian artists found inspiration in the flying deities of ancient faiths

By GILBERT HIGHET

With Gloria In Excelsis Deo *on their lips, the angels of the Lord hover directly above the Manger
in this detail of Ghirlandaio's* Adoration of the Magi *(1488) in the Foundling Hospital, Florence.*

After we emerged from the cave, we looked up to the sky. Ever since then we have been trying to reach it.

The artists and mystics of the early and middle Stone Ages watched animals, modeled animals, drew animals, dreamed about animals, and in hours of worship, themselves became animals. Animals still remain deep in our hearts, as friends or competitors or victims. But after our civilization began, in the flat plains along the rich rivers, our ideal changed from the swift-running foot to the high-soaring wing. We thought less of the forests than of the clouds. God's voice was no longer the growl in the jungle but the roar in the sky. God moved no longer in the galloping pack and in the terrible prowler, but in the thunderheads which held the furious lightning and in the mountain which jetted flame and shook the earth. God's messengers, God's companions, God himself now dwelt in the heavens, and when they visited mankind, they flew down from great heights and soared back again.

The men of the Middle Eastern lands gazed at the sky with keen, thoughtful, devout eyes. They built lofty temples, rising by steps of sanctity away from the earth. Their gods were stars and planets, or dwelt among the stars and planets; the spirits, intermediary between divinity and humanity, had wings so that they might pass easily from this low world into heaven. The Assyrian monarch's palace, for example, was guarded by bulls—symbols of primacy, energy, and masculinity—but the bulls had the bearded faces of men, because they were intelligent, and they had wings, because they were emanations of God. On the monuments describing the king's glory, his divine attendants were spirits: men in face and beard and body and costume but wearing the wings of huge birds. The sun had sent them down to earth. They carried the sun through the heavens, bearing his life-giving disk like a jewel in their hands. When they came to earth, they fertilized the palms and brought the date harvest, that recurrent miracle which built the king's prosperity and the happiness of his people.

It was from the Assyrians that the Greeks learned how to portray a spirit as a man or woman with wings (page 33).

27

The earliest of all Greek poems and works of art show us some mysterious sacred birds, and some gods and goddesses who change into birds for a moment after an epiphany. Now the great Greek gods have no wings. Wings would degrade them. Apollo shooting the arrows of the sun, Artemis bending the moon-bow, Athena wearing the tempest as a breastplate, Zeus driving clouds and brandishing the thunderbolt —these inhabit the regions of heaven as naturally as men walk the low earth: their dwelling is the sky-touching peak of Mount Olympus, unscalable and sacred. But other deities are winged. The messenger of the gods, Hermes, who must often travel between earth and sky, earth and underworld, has wings: not on his shoulders but, as a delicate and almost inessential appendage, upon his heels. The fast-flying spirit of passionate love, Eros, is depicted by the Greeks as a capricious boy of twelve or thirteen, handsome, cruel, enchanting, naked, and confident, with a powerful span of rapid wings on his bare shoulders. And another spirit, who is to politics what Eros is to personal life, has two great wings. She is the desirable, evasive, unpredictable deity who, with calmly smiling face, hovers like a noonday cloud above a battlefield bitter with blows and groans, and then, while the vanquished melt into heaps of corpses and sullen gangs of slaves, glides down a sunbeam to bring glory to the panting conquerors. She is among the fairest of all Greek images of the divine: the Winged Victory. Throughout the world of Greece and Rome, Victory flew from conquest to conquest, sometimes visiting upstart empires like that of Athens, sometimes settling upon powerful monarchies like those of Alexander and his successors, sometimes flaunted by doomed Roman revolutionaries, and finally identified with the protecting goddess of the Roman city and state. We can still see her as she was when the Greek and Roman artists captured a glimpse of her and made her into marble (page 34), standing tiptoe on the pediment of a temple or holding forth her crown from the prow of a battleship, with proud breast bare and wings still flickering from her rapid descent from heaven.

The Jews, on the other hand, clung and cling to the great idea that God cannot be seen. He resembles no thing and no animal and no man. He is a spirit, indescribable and unnamable. Although he has a voice and has often been heard speaking, still "no man hath seen God." In the Old Testament, God sends his people many messengers ("angel" is simply the Greek word for "messenger"), but although their power and their mission are supernatural, they themselves are not winged. The two angels who visited Lot before the destruction of Sodom looked like ordinary men. They were treated by Lot simply as distinguished foreign guests, whom he saved from the insults of the Sodomites. In one of the most mysterious episodes of the Bible, a stranger wrestled with Jacob all night at a ford, beat him by throwing his thigh out of joint, hurried away before sunrise, refused to state his name, and gave Jacob a new name meaning "Wrestler with God"—Israel. Jacob said his opponent was God himself; later interpreters believe it was an angel. In any case, the wrestler appeared to Jacob simply as a man.

In the most beautiful episodes related in the New Testament, the messengers of God are not said to have wings. In Luke's Gospel, the angel Gabriel foretells to the Jewish priest Zacharias the birth of his son John the Baptist, and to Mary, the betrothed of Joseph, the birth of her son Jesus, the King of Israel. To Zacharias, Gabriel appears standing beside the altar of the temple at Jerusalem. To Mary he "comes in" at Nazareth, and from her he merely "departs." After the appointed time arrived, the shepherds in the country around Bethlehem were visited by a messenger who "came upon them" in the night, to tell them of the birth of the Saviour. *And suddenly there was with the angel a multitude of the heavenly host praising God, and saying, "Glory to God in the highest, and on earth peace, good will toward men."* After this unique moment, the angels "were gone away from them into heaven." We are told nothing of their outward appearance. We are not told that they had wings—or indeed that they attended on the birth of Jesus and sang above the stable where he was cradled. And after the death of Jesus, when Mary Magdalene and her companions went to the grave to anoint his corpse, they were met, not by figures which flew through the air, but by "a young man sitting [in the tomb] clothed in a long white garment" or by "two men [who] stood by them in shining garments." The words of Scripture are clear, austere, pure. God's emissaries speak the language of men; they utter a plain, powerful message; they have the shape natural for human beings, or else they are left undescribed.

How is it, then, that whenever we hear the word "angel," we see a being with large wings? How is it that the image in our minds is a graceful shape with flowing robes and floating hair and kindly gaze, sexless or almost sexless, or perhaps with a hint of the feminine? God's messenger Gabriel, who spoke so authoritatively to Zacharias and Mary, was evidently masculine in form and nature. But painters have often depicted the angel of the Annunciation (see detail from Fra Angelico's fresco on page 35) as a gentle visitor, like a maid of honor sent to pay homage to a princess; and the angel does not "come in" to Mary's room but flies down from heaven on a pair of birdlike wings.

This is because Christian art is a blend of Jewish mysticism and Greek imagery. The Jews, for whom the Old Testament and much of the New Testament were written, thought

In Western iconography the dragon is a writhing symbol of evil, even of the Devil himself. But to the Chinese it is a benevolent heavenly spirit, a defender of mankind. The cloud-borne dragons at the left are from a scroll painted by the Sung artist Chen Jung about 1235–40.

of God as being free of all bodily form and his messengers as human in appearance—mediums or diplomats, as it were, characterless save for their mission. But the Greeks, or at least the Greek artists and poets, could not think of the divine as formless, with no resemblance to humanity. To them, a god wore the shape of a perfect man or woman, endowed with superhuman powers. And the messenger of divinity must surely have the appurtenances of swift and graceful flight. Therefore Christian artists, working in the Graeco-Roman tradition, gave their angels the wings of Victory and Eros and the Genius. But this did not happen all at once. Before the change was made, there was a long period of doubt and resistance. When the change did come, it was part of the great conversion of the pagan world.

The earliest Christian artists portray Jesus neither as an individual with distinctive features nor as a rabbi. Instead, they show him as one of the symbolic figures established by the vivid Greek imagination: Orpheus, teacher and poet, Hermes the friendly deity, carrying a lamb on his shoulders. In the same way, during the first four Christian centuries, angels are not shown as having wings. They are (as in the Scriptures) handsome youths, beardless, wearing ordinary clothes (ankle-length gown and cloak), standing or moving humanly upon the ground. But this was scarcely satisfactory. Artists wanted to distinguish the heavenly messengers from other young male figures such as the disciples of Jesus and Jesus himself. Greek and Roman Christian poets, elaborating on the Gospel stories, introduced traditional classical imagery. Thus, the good Paulinus of Nola, after describing the angel Gabriel's visit to Zacharias, concludes with something which is not in the Scriptures: "He spoke, and glided on wings into thin air." Mystics and divines reflected on the strange powers given by the Almighty to his envoys—their

sudden appearances and disappearances, their rapid movement, their ubiquity—and concluded that, although human in form, they must be superhuman both in their beauty and in their power of flight.

About A.D. 400, after long suspense and mounting pressure, an ancient and enormous dam broke. The waters of the Christian spirit gushed into dry pagan channels, filling them with new energy and reviving much of the moribund life along their banks. Again and again, then and thereafter, we see pagan philosophical ideas, aesthetic patterns, imaginative symbols, and social and religious customs taken over by Christianity, rededicated and, without destruction, transformed. One of the oldest houses of worship in existence is the cathedral of Syracuse. It is simply the temple of Athena, built five centuries before Christ, and after twelve hundred years of paganism, converted into a Christian church. In the same way, the angels of Jewish and Christian Scripture took on the wings, the grace, and the spiritual intensity of Graeco-Roman spirits and demigods.

In Greek and Roman belief, an unseen guardian accompanies each of us from birth to death and (as Menander says) "initiates us into the mystic rites of life." He is our daemon, or our Genius. On sculptured tombs, the Genius sometimes appears at the moment of death, extinguishing his torch or, as the soul, flying away from the funeral pyre into heaven. This kindly companion gave his wings and something of his personality to the Christian angels.

The image of Victory had always accompanied the Roman emperors. When they, too, became Christians, she did not leave them. In the imperial palace at Constantinople, the emperor's throne was flanked by two Victories with outspread wings, each holding a laurel crown. In Christian churches, too, the winged Victories now appeared, carrying the palms of triumph—as they did for Greek athletes at the great games, as the Jews did when they greeted Christ at his entry into Jerusalem, and as the blessed do standing before the throne of God in the Revelation of Saint John. In one strange, mystical picture from northern Italy, we see a procession centering on a winged female figure who stands beside a basket of bread and a cup of wine. The spirit is Victory, the bread and wine symbolize Jesus; and the two together mean *Christos Nika*, "Christ is Victorious!"

So it is that just as Greek and Roman temples became Christian houses of worship, just as subtle Greek philosophical thought and strong Roman organizing power were transfused into the Church, just as the wealth and vigor of Greek rhetoric and Roman poetry were put to the service of the new religion, so the messengers, the guardians, and the heavenly visitors of Graeco-Roman paganism gave their flight, their dignity, and their charm to the angels of Christian art and literature.

Much was taken, but much was rejected. In particular, pagan sensuality was utterly rejected. Eros and the Genius were male and naked. Victory was female and lightly clad. When Victory entered the Church, she might still soar, but she was decorously clothed; and all the angels were masculine, grave of aspect, and fully clad. For the early Christians, the beauty of the body was a snare and a delusion if it was not the outward semblance, and only the semblance, of spiritual holiness.

But in the Renaissance, ten centuries later, pagan Greece and Rome asserted themselves. The human body, so long shrouded and contemned that its beauties, almost its shape, had been forgotten, was revealed once more for artists to paint and carve and for the world to enjoy. Thenceforward, although the angels were never naked, they were more delicately draped, so that the line and rhythm of their handsome bodies were sometimes disclosed. Their wings glowed and glittered with the vivid hues of a peacock's fan. Their faces became softer, more winning, more humanly expressive in rapture, in grief, in wonder, or in worship. In the hands of painters and sculptors trained by admiring and copying Greek statuary, the angels reverted more emphatically to the pagan part of their ancestry (see detail from Ghirlandaio's *Adoration of the Magi*, pages 26–27).

Even the god of love now reappeared among them. As Eros, the gay, cruel stripling, he was still impossible for Christians to use in religious art. But the later Greeks themselves had diminished and multiplied Eros into a swarm of playful children, the Erotes or Cupids, who are often shown engaged in inappropriate but amusing adult occupations (pages 36–37), and often, like modern Italian children in a procession, merely dance along carrying garlands and strew-

ing flowers. These Cupids were now converted and enlisted in the Christian host of heaven. Their unabashed nakedness, suitable both to babies and to pagans, was circumvented. They were clothed in wisps of ribbon or discreetly posed; and sometimes their embarrassingly frank little bodies were simply abolished, so that they became chubby infant heads with wings. So the Cupids became, as it were, pages in the royal court of God. On occasions of rejoicing they played instruments and sang (see frieze on bottom of pages 36–37). They joined in aerial ceremonies, carrying processional garlands, or themselves forming a floating cloudlike garland of infant adorers. And sometimes, as in Raphael's lovely painting of the Madonna and Child, they attended on their infant prince, watching him in his mother's arms with awe and admiration and love.

From Jerome to Thomas Aquinas, Christian divines had earnestly discussed the problem of angels' flight. In the Renaissance, artists took up this problem in their own way. Not many of them attempted to solve it by studying real winged creatures in flight—partly, no doubt, because few of them had the inquiring mind and sharp eyes of Leonardo, and partly because they felt it would be inappropriate and even irreverent. Some solved it in the simplest way. To show that an angel was in flight, they spread his wings, let his feet hang without the upward pressure of the ground, and suspended him as though swinging gently in mid-air, with the landscape far beneath him. This was appropriate for angels at rest, singing above the Bethlehem stable or poised in a glory at the Transfiguration or the Ascension. Other artists, who had to show angels in rapid movement, did so either by copying the rhythms of a swimmer—since the freedom of movement in liquid is closer to the motion of flight than the earthbound gestures of walking—or else by virtually ignoring the force of gravity and treating the bodies, wings, and draperies of angels like currents of vapor or moving arabesques of cloud, borne up, flexed, and played with by a light invisible wind.

We are often told that the Greek imagination excels in its power to make nature animate and personal: to hear the laughter of a nymph in the ripple of every wave and to make every tempestuous flooded river a charging bull. But the fantasies of the East are quite as fertile. Long before Buddha was born, the Indians peopled the sky with nymphs, the Apsarases. These charming creatures resemble Aphrodite in both name and nature. Born of water, they live in the sky, floating through mid-air in bright, multicolored garments, upheld and drawn hither and thither by their floating scarves and flying draperies (see page 38). They sing and play, although we human beings cannot hear their music. Being flexible and feminine, they never resist, and indeed invite, the amorous male deities. And sometimes, when an ascetic, through many years of self-torment, is about to attain such sanctity that he will possess superhuman powers, the Apsarases will descend to earth, seduce him, and disappear again into bright illusion. They are the clouds.

In Jewish and Christian thought there are not only good angels but evil angels. These last, once the servants of God, though fallen are still mighty. Since they were once heavenly beings, they have wings; since they rebelled against God and rejected his gifts, they have been transformed into figures as hideous as they were formerly beautiful. Once noble, the devils are now foul and grotesque (pages 44 and 45). The tragic Satan whom Milton describes as looking like the sun in a cloudy dawn or the moon in eclipse—sad but sublime—is not the devil as conceived by most Christian poets, artists, and thinkers: for there is still something left in him to admire, even to pity. No, Satan is either the cruel tempter, jester, and liar of *Job* and *Faust* or a monster like the Lucifer whom Dante saw at the very root of hell: with three faces—black, red, and pallid yellow—three mouths chewing the bodies of archsinners, and three pairs of wings, not like those worn by angels but like those of night-flying, blood-sucking bats,

and he was flapping them
to make three separate blasts of icy wind.

Hatred, not pity; disgust, not admiration; yes, and fear—these are the three cold emotions which are stirred in most poets and artists by the sight, the very thought, of the foul fiend and his angels. The demon Malacoda, who meets Dante and Vergil beside the lake of boiling tar, tells his subordinates to escort the poets farther on their journey. They acknowledge his command by sticking out their tongues, like gargoyles, "and he then made a trumpet of his rump." This distortion of the dignity which even men share with true angels is merely hateful; but a few hundred paces farther, the demons grow savage and threatening, and Dante clings to Vergil like a child to its mother.

This is the terror which Jacques Callot depicted in his *Temptation of St. Anthony* (pages 44–45). Young men, distracted by their new sexual urge, often imagine that the worst affliction of the saints was their enforced celibacy, the worst temptation visions of beautiful, naked, accessible women. But the hardest temptation for many saints has been the sense of hopeless terror in the presence of real, powerful, strong-willed, all but ubiquitous evil. And so, in Callot's picture (and in that by Hieronymus Bosch, which surely helped to inspire it), we see the wretched saint alone, with no church, no sanctuary, no visible companion, surrounded and all but overwhelmed by the forces of unreason and utter disorganization, dominated for a time at least by the Prince of the Powers of the Air.

In Christian thought, the evil one has power only upon this earth, and only for a time. It is strange, therefore, to look at heaven through Eastern eyes and to see it filled with apparitions of terror, ferocity, and madness. In the West, the dragon is the Loathly Worm that lies coiled in its cave, defending its treasure with poison fangs and fiery breath; it is the evil monster killed by the god Apollo or by Saint George; it is the scarlet beast of Revelation, upon which rides the harlot drunken with the blood of the martyrs; it is the Devil himself, writhing under the spear of the warrior archangel Michael. But in China the dragon is a kindly spirit inhabiting the realms of the air and defending mankind against far more dangerous demons. And a Tibetan paradise, although it is the heaven to which Tibetan souls aspire and is surrounded by flying nymphs and bright rainbows and cloudy emanations of the divine, still contains such fearful figures as Sen-ge sgra-sgrogs, a savior whose body is blue, who wears a tiger skin and a garland of human heads, and who brandishes the thunderbolt (page 39). Power and fear, rather than nobility and love, are the attributes of divinity in such a heaven.

Until this present era, most mere human beings have lived and moved upon or beneath the surface of the earth. But in every land a few have been believed capable of rising above it and, for a time at least, of soaring toward heaven without wings. This is the phenomenon called levitation. When it occurs, the gross human body, with its thick flesh and bones, which pulls us down toward the center of this heavy globe, becomes weightless. It rises into the middle air and rests there like a cloud. Sometimes, like a great but wingless bird, it flies from place to place through the air. In the West the most famous levitator was the Franciscan Saint Joseph of Copertine (1603–1663), whose passionate religious ecstasies used to draw him soaring through the church, high above the ground. Sometimes carrying his confessor with him, he was observed to fly as far as thirty yards. Joseph was seen flying by the Pope himself, Urban VIII; and a duke of the house of Brunswick was so overwhelmed by the spectacle that he gave up his Protestant faith for Roman Catholicism. The Holy Office of the Inquisition viewed Joseph's ethereal raptures with grave mistrust, banished him from Rome to Assisi, and when his miraculous flights did not cease, expelled him from Assisi, too; but his powers continued until death.

Mystics of other lands also have soared into the air. But

in the Far East, passion has no place in higher religion, so that levitating saints are more tranquil. Seated in the pose of meditation, they rise above the earth to meet the shrine's floating deity (page 47) or, like Chinese sages, walk among the clouds in converse with the immortal spirits (page 46).

There are, it would seem, several means of achieving this mystical wingless flight. Magic is not among them; it is merely vulgar superstition that makes the Chinese say their holy men rise on "fishskin shoes." Foremost is the desire for union with the divine. To this union, the heavy body of humanity is an almost invincible obstacle. In ecstasy a contemplative will sometimes become unconscious, almost ceasing to live physically. Sometimes (although less frequently) his aspiring spirit will carry the body with it away from earth.

In both the East and the West special powers have always been attributed to the man who, by the long practice of ascetic self-denial and the calm endurance of extreme self-inflicted suffering, has made his body not the tyrant which it is for most people nor the companion of the soul which it is for some but a thing more obedient than a slave, more passive than a garment. Levitation, impossible for others, seems, for a body thus tamed and dominated, to be effortless.

In the East another method, strange to us, is recognized. For many Oriental sages, all the material world is illusion, and only the spiritual is real. To make this drastic statement is easy; but to arrive at full understanding of it takes long years of meditation. When it is truly understood, then passing through physical obstacles, performing what others think miracles, and rising into the air—these are simple, almost unimportant acts. As the Taoist mystic Shan Ch'iu Kai said, "When the mind becomes One, then material objects offer no resistance."

Both in philosophy and in religion, then, we often find that the utmost effort and almost the utmost reward are to rise above this earth toward the supramundane realm of the sky. This visionary experience lies close to the heart of two great world faiths. The founder of Islam, Mohammed the Prophet, mounted on the miraculous steed Burak, spanned the spheres in one night, until, alone of human beings, he visited heaven and returned to dwell for a time on earth. And in the greatest of all Christian poems we may still journey with Dante, first into the interior of this sinful earth, through hell, then laboriously up the antipodean mountain of Purgatory, and finally, in a series of magnificent visions, past moon and sun and planets into the Deep Heaven of space, where God dwells among his blessed and his angels.

ANGELS and ANTECEDENTS

A PORTFOLIO OF BENIGN (AND SOME SATANIC) SPIRITS

On the following pages HORIZON *presents the evolution, if the word is permissible, of the angel—from the guardian spirits of the Assyrians, winged but still somehow earthbound, to the radiant and wholly aerial seraphim of Renaissance art. Along the way are some Oriental mutations—flying saints and celestial nymphs—who are not dependent on wings. This is an Eastern idea; the West has usually insisted on giving its heavenly messengers the visible apparatus of flight. Thus in the ninth century* B.C., *the Assyrians put wings on the shoulders of their protective geniuses, even though their heavy, muscle-bound bodies and squarely planted feet seem to belong irrevocably to the earth. The one opposite, who is shown fertilizing the blossoms of the date palm, is from the palace of the great King Ashur-Nasir-Pal II at Nimrud in what is now Iraq.*

Victory, with her splendid wings
and floating draperies, moved from the
Greek and Roman pantheon into the
Christian—to lend her shape to heavenly messengers—with some changes.
Like the third-century example above
from Leptis Magna in Libya, she was
too lightly clad for early Christians.
Recoiling from this pagan nakedness,
pre-Renaissance painters such as Fra
Angelico (detail of his Annunciation
opposite) modestly robed their angels.

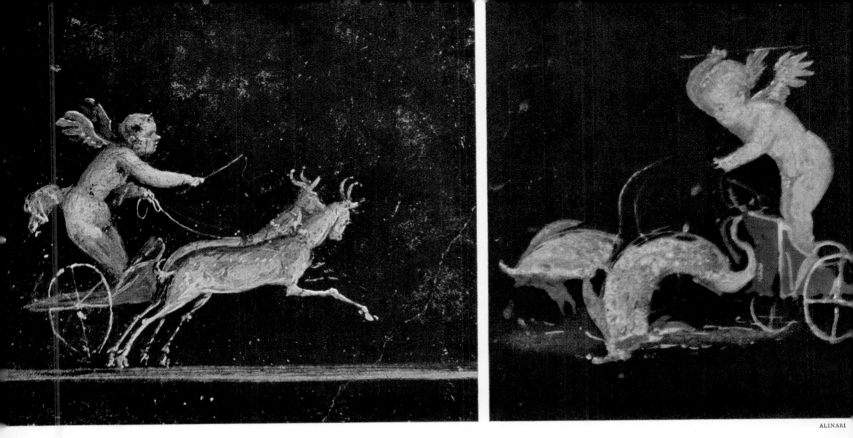

Eros, the god of love, was at first a lithe but lone adolescent. The later Greeks and Romans multiplied him into a band of playful Cupids, like the amorini *above from the House of the Vettii in Pompeii. After losing a few years and acquiring more suitable occupations, such as music-making, they found their way into the heavenly host—becoming the cherubim of the French baroque altarpiece below, at Champagny in Savoy.*

The artists of Japan suggested the flight of an Apsaras by the liquid swirl of her draperies. The one above, made of lacquered wood, was carved sometime between the ninth and twelfth centuries. She is not unlike the celestial nymphs in the Tibetan paradise opposite, who may be seen flying just inside the rainbow. This eighteenth-century banner depicts, with the most complex symbolism, the struggle to achieve salvation. In the center sits the great teacher Padmasambhava, surrounded by his two foremost women disciples and the eight gurus (or teachers) who were his previous incarnations. The one just below him and slightly to the left is the fearful blue-bodied Sen-ge sgra-sgrogs. At the bottom are two ropelike bridges on which human souls are precariously crossing from earth to the paradise of Padmasambhava.

38

The wings of Persian angels are often fragile and many-hued, like those of the peri in the sixteenth-century miniature above, or of the angels on the opposite page. In this seventeenth-century miniature of Mohammed's ascent, the veiled Prophet—astride the steed Burak—makes his passage across the sky, strewn with stars and signs of the Zodiac, to the farthest circle of heaven.

41

*O*f Jacob's meeting with the angel, above, the Bible says only, "And Jacob
was left alone; and there wrestled a man with him until the breaking of the
day." There is no hint here that the stranger was anything but fully human
in appearance. But Christian artists were determined to show that the heavenly adversary was physically, as well as spiritually, different from Jacob;
so they furnished him with a pair of majestic wings, as in this thirteenth-
century mosaic from the Basilica of Monreale in Sicily. Equally regal is
the figure of Saint Michael the Archangel on the Byzantine icon opposite.
It was brought to Venice by crusaders who pillaged Constantinople in 1204.

*C*hristianity also created fallen angels. The traditional image of Satan was established by Duccio di Buoninsegna's Temptation of Christ, above. After that, devils were almost invariably given batlike wings, as in the detail below from Signorelli's Last Judgment or as in this pandemonium imagined by the seventeenth-century French etcher Jacques Callot in The Temptation of St. Anthony, opposite.

*A*lthough Oriental art is full of heavenly visitants, their arrivals and departures are usually made without benefit of wings. In the painting above, which is from an early fourteenth-century Japanese scroll, the deity of the Kasuga shrine in Nara has come down from the clouds to converse with a mortal. The deity has manifested itself in the guise of a princess wearing full Japanese court dress, and the sense of wonder is intensified by the fact that both figures appear to be floating. Even more patently miraculous is the flying Taoist saint in the Chinese drawing opposite (Ming period, 1368–1644). He may be wearing a pair of the legendary fishskin "flying cloud shoes," but it is more likely that he has achieved the Taoist holy man's ambition of flying skyward by starving himself to weightlessness.

OVERLEAF: God descends from heaven, trailing a cloud of angels, in this detail from one of Ghiberti's celebrated doors for the Baptistry in Florence.

By GERMAINE BRÉE

The Innocent Amusements of Jean Anouilh

Claiming that he is only diverting himself, this front-rank dramatist attracts many people and exasperates others with an array of ironic plays whose wry and sometimes jarring air is not so innocent after all

Whenever the French playwright Jean Anouilh gets around to publishing a few of his plays (he is a prodigal writer, and there are now more than two dozen of them), he accommodatingly classifies them for his readers. But instead of using the conventional tags of comedy, tragedy, or farce, he willfully calls them *pièces roses, noires, brillantes,* or *grinçantes*—"pink," "black," "brilliant," or "jarring" plays. Perhaps it is just this lack of a familiar label that baffles Broadway audiences, for the most successful playwright in France has nòt had a commensurate success in America.

It is certainly not for want of exposure; the opening of *Becket* on Broadway this fall marks the eleventh play of his to be given a New York production in the past fifteen years (Tennessee Williams is the only other living playwright who can match that record). The first half dozen or so were failures, and it was not until 1955, with his Joan of Arc play, *The Lark,* that he had a real Broadway success. Even after that, despite the generally favorable reception of *The Waltz of the Toreadors, Time Remembered,* and *The Fighting Cock,* the attitude of both public and critics has remained moody, ambivalent, and detached. "So far as I'm concerned," a New York critic was saying only a couple of years ago, "Anouilh and ennui are the same thing." It remains to be seen whether *Becket* will exercise the same fascination in New York that it has, for more than a year, in Paris; but with Anthony Quinn playing the truculent, barbaric Norman king, Henry Plantagenet, and Laurence Olivier as Thomas à Becket, his elegant, aristocratic friend and enemy, it would seem that Anouilh has at least survived the critic's pun.

Colette, France's great *femme de lettres,* once shrewdly remarked, "It seems to me that the critics are mad at Anouilh just because they enjoy his theater so much." Even now, Anouilh—who at fifty is more vigorously productive than ever before—cannot count on the critics' reactions from one play to the next. "Watch out," he is reported to have said when *The Lark* was starting out on its triumphant Paris run, "I've only been paroled."

Anouilh is often berated in the French press. He does very little to ingratiate himself with his critics; he is well known for his deep dislike of publicity, and besides, he doesn't take the press very seriously. He has on occasion recalled the unwelcome role of drama critics even in his childhood. His mother, using one of the critics of the day as a bogeyman, would say, "Jean, if you don't eat your soup, I'll call Le Cardonnel!" And when *Becket* opened in Paris last year, he wrote, "I have long since stopped trying to defend myself. . . . My critics should know once and for all . . . that I respect their indignation, that I sometimes exasperate myself just as much as I exasperate them, but that I have not the slightest intention of mending my ways." And so he continues, with complete equanimity, to pile success upon failure upon success in all the theaters of the Western world.

He seems to be more of an actors' and producers' playwright than a critics' play-

Anouilh supervises a scene in the Paris production of his Becket, *a play about the ideological duel between Thomas à Becket and Henry Plantagenet. It is visiting Broadway this fall.*

wright. Since 1932, when Pierre Fresnay (an excellent and popular actor of the time) played the leading role in *The Ermine,* his first serious play, Anouilh has had the knack of attracting front-rank figures in the theater. In France there have been Georges Pitoëff (who launched him on the road to success), André Barsacq, and Jean-Louis Barrault. In America it was Katharine Cornell who, with *Antigone,* in 1946, really introduced New York theatergoers to Anouilh. Since then, Christopher Fry's brilliant translation of *Ring Round the Moon,* Julie Harris in Lillian Hellman's adaptation of *The Lark,* Helen Hayes in *Time Remembered,* Sir Ralph Richardson in *The Waltz of the Toreadors,* and Rex Harrison in *The Fighting Cock* have all shown how strongly Anouilh appeals to a wide variety of eminent theater people.

This is understandable. He is a man who has lived all his life in and for the theater. His mother belonged to that innumerable crowd of humble theater folk—third- or fourth-rate *artistes*—who live from hand to mouth as they move uneasily between the glamour of the theater and the dismal, mediocre reality of their difficult off-stage lives. They haunt Anouilh's plays, and no doubt they gave him one of his insights into the nature of human beings: his awareness of their disarming addiction to illusion. Many of his plays are concerned with a very human problem translated into theatrical terms: how to grow into adulthood without turning into a kind of fourth-rate actor whose pathetic play acting is as apparent to himself as it is to others.

Anouilh's most cherished memories—at least the only ones of which he speaks—are always related to the theater. Perhaps the most extraordinary of all is the memory of a season spent in Arcachon, a summer resort in southwest France, when he was eight. For three months, he went every night to the Casino but never stayed beyond the intermission—his bedtime. Thus he never learned the fate reserved for the glittering operetta characters on the stage, characters whose off-stage lives he knew all too well. But from that experience he feels he derived a sense of dramatic rhythm, an insight into the nature of a stage character's role, and a feeling for the properly theatrical as distinguished from the literary. It is these qualities that prompted the poet John Ciardi to write, "Of all the playwrights I know of in modern times, Anouilh has the surest sense of the stage."

Certainly it takes a wonderful, imaginative sense of the stage to create and project such memorable scenes as the climactic one in *Becket.* The play is named for the martyred Archbishop of Canterbury whose fate is also the subject of T. S. Eliot's *Murder in the Cathedral.* Toward the end, Becket meets Henry Plantagenet, his erstwhile companion and close friend from whom he is now estranged, in an effort at reconciliation. They confront each other on horseback, in the middle of a plain in northern France. The two actors, raised high on invisible wooden clogs under the heavy caparisons of their imitation horses, are set upon a stage marked off in black and white squares: king and bishop, the chess-

Anouilh's World in America

Above: Julie Harris (as Joan of Arc) addresses Christopher Plummer (Warwick) in The Lark.
Below: Lucile Watson makes a point to her butler in Ring Round the Moon.

VANDAMM

Below: Katharine Cornell is restrained by a pair of bully boys in Antigone, *the first of Anouilh's plays to reach Broadway (1946).*

VANDAMM

Above: In Time Remembered *Susan Strasberg is looking for a ride, but that ivied taxi is used only to house rabbits.*

Below: Ralph Richardson as General Saint-Pé succors his nagging wife (Mildred Natwick) in The Waltz of the Toreadors.

SHELDON SECUNDA

HERB NOTT, TORONTO

Above: Rex Harrison delivers a harangue in The Fighting Cock, *a play in which the chief character is another of Anouilh's fatuous generals.*

53

men in "God's game" (the subtitle of *Becket* is "The Honor of God"). The visual effect is powerful and highly dramatic. But then, each of Anouilh's plays has brought its own unexpected setting: the bare stage and black tuxedos of *Antigone*; the enchanted never-never land of the "sleeping prince" in *Time Remembered*; the medieval court of justice in *The Lark* where Joan's trial takes place and which evokes successively all the traditional décors of her life, giving way at last to the grandeur of the coronation scene at Rheims.

Skill, certainly, and more than skill—an innate sense of theater. Married to an actress, Monelle Valentin, who sometimes creates leading parts in her husband's plays, Anouilh also has an actress daughter, Catherine. To divert the guests at his daughter's wedding, Anouilh wrote one of his most charming comedies, *The School for Fathers*, in which Catherine later starred. But the family's experience of the theater has not always been attended by such lighthearted virtuosity. When they married, both he and Monelle Valentin were penniless. He was the poorly paid secretary of Louis Jouvet, one of France's outstanding actors and directors during the period between the wars, and Monelle had no job at all. Jouvet had little respect for the attempts of his down-at-the-heels secretary to be a dramatist and disdainfully rejected all his plays. So this young couple who could not break into the theater ironically began their life together amidst stage sets: their only furniture was some props borrowed from Jouvet's production of Giraudoux's *Siegfried*. Since there was no baby in the play, and consequently no cradle, Catherine Anouilh spent her first weeks in a suitcase.

Poverty accompanied Anouilh for many years; it may have given him the burning sense of justice known to his friends, and it certainly supplied him with one of his characteristic themes. Not that Anouilh's heroes revolt against poverty for purely materialistic reasons: poverty for them is daily degradation—the sure path to humiliation, pettiness, resignation, and bitterness. In *The Ermine*, the penniless young hero tells the girl he loves (who has a wealthy aunt) that he won't marry her if it forces them both to live in poverty:

FRANTZ: I love you, Monime.
MONIME: Why are you afraid then?
FRANTZ: Because I love you. Because I know what petty things can kill the greatest love. . . .
MONIME: We are strong enough to fight them.
FRANTZ: Not with poverty to fight as well. Poverty will line up with our enemies. . . . You don't know the way that poverty goes to work; how ingenious it is—how persistent. For twenty years now I have had it at my heels like a snarling dog—I know that nothing can resist it, even youth, although youth is as vital and as strong as love. I'm afraid of it. I'm afraid of the beautiful women we shall pretend not to notice when you are poor and ill dressed. . . . I'm afraid of seeing you diminish every day—taking orders from a boss or doing sordid chores about the house.

Rather than give up his love or submit Monime to the daily ordeal by poverty, Frantz makes up his mind to kill the rich aunt—a new and very modern Raskolnikov in revolt against the injustices of a society that makes money the prerequisite to realizing one's most disinterested and legitimate aspirations. But poverty in Anouilh's world cuts even more deeply than that, as Thérèse, the twenty-year-old heroine of *Restless Heart*, discovers. The daughter of aging, unsuccessful *artistes*, Thérèse is loved by Florent—gentle, charming, talented, wealthy young Florent. As the play progresses, she sees her own world of soiled, promiscuous, servile human beings enveloping Florent, entering with her into his beautiful, ordered, kindly home. Her revolt and despair are violent:

THÉRÈSE: You are a rich man. . . . A conqueror who never fought a battle.
FLORENT: But you can't go on forever blaming me for my money. What do you expect me to do with it?
THÉRÈSE: Oh, nothing, Florent. You could throw it all to the winds, laughing, the way you did the other day, but my pain wouldn't vanish with it. You aren't only rich in money, you see, you're rich in the house where you grew up, rich in your life's deep peace and the age-old tranquillity of your forefathers. You're rich in your joy of living that never had to attack or defend itself, and in your talent too. . . . You know nothing! That's what hurts the most! It's your privilege to know nothing!

Almost all of Anouilh's early plays have this common theme, a revolt against the material and moral squalor bred by poverty. Even in so late a play as *Becket*, this attitude is present in the king's contempt for the family of peasants in whose hut he and Becket have been forced to take shelter:

THE KING: . . . (*Regarding the man with exasperation.*) Look at that. It's dumb, it's obtuse, it proliferates, it stinks, it's all over the place. (*He catches the girl as she tries to get away.*) Stay here! Of what use is it, do you think?
BECKET: It scratches the earth, it makes bread. . . .
THE KING: The curious thing about it is that it is so ugly and produces such pretty girls. How do you account for that, you who can account for everything?
BECKET: At twenty, before he lost his teeth and took on that indefinable age of the masses, he was perhaps handsome. Perhaps he had one night of love, one minute when he too was king and forgot his terror. After that, his life of misery took over as before. His wife and he probably forgot. But the seed was cast.
THE KING: . . . (*Looking at the girl.*) You think she'll become as ugly as the others?
BECKET: Certainly.

It has often been said that his heroes refuse happiness when it is offered to them. That is not strictly true. What they refuse is a happiness made up of petty resignation, of mean compensations snatched from life with humiliating eagerness. As Orpheus, in *Legend of Lovers*, goes to his death out of the hideous fly-stained room where, the day before, he had shared with Eurydice the pure enchantment of love, his father talks of "life": of casual sexual adventures, of cheap meals gluttonously enjoyed, of all the small change of pleasure allotted to the unwanted, wandering, penny-counting musician that he is. Poverty is not an abstract social theme for Anouilh, nor does he treat it as such. It is, in fact, an insidious criminal, and it sets the stage for many

Taunted that he still loves Thomas à Becket, the king roars at the Bishop of London (in the Paris production of Anouilh's Becket*): "Yes, I love him! But that's no business of yours, Curé. I have confided to you only my hate. I am going to pay you to get rid of him, but never speak ill of him to me!"*

of the plots against human integrity and happiness that are the subject of Anouilh's *pièces noires*.

It was the theater that saved Anouilh from the dead end of poverty. In a television interview, Moss Hart once recalled his violent hatred of the poverty he knew as a young man, and how—after his first success in the theater—he opened wide all the windows of his miserable apartment and let the rain beat in to obliterate, to purify, to wash out the poverty. Anouilh's own gesture was less dramatic, but the impulse was similar; with the first money he made as a playwright, he bought a small blue convertible and carried his wife off in triumph under the unbelieving eyes of the concierge—ever suspicious, naturally, of the goings-on of the "poor."

Even before it saved him materially, the theater had sustained him spiritually. The dog-eared copies of Claudel, Shaw, and Pirandello that he carried in his pocket fascinated him, but it was Jean Giraudoux who, in fact, revealed to him the world of drama. That was in the spring of 1928, when *Siegfried*, Giraudoux's first play, opened at the Comédie des Champs-Elysées. It spelled enchantment for Anouilh, "warming" the Avenue Montaigne, "bringing it into flower." With a sardonic reference to the theater's fashionable location, he later wrote to Giraudoux: "Though others have found their poetry in the quiet streets of a sleepy town, along the banks of a still lake . . . in a poetic setting, my poetry was to have its rendezvous with me, because of you, in that Parisian landscape for rich foreigners with its accessory figures scarcely suited to please me."

For Anouilh, the stage had always been a magical and poetic world, but Giraudoux gave him something more: the first intimation that it might be for him, too, a means of communication with others. "In the years around 1928," he continued, "I was all alone. Alone with all the anguish of one soon to be twenty years old, with a love for the theater, and all the awkwardness of youth. . . . it is because of those spring evenings [at the time of *Siegfried*] that I have been able to move somewhat out of myself."

A quiet little man, reserved and rather unapproachable despite the large, light, gray-blue eyes that peer benignly from behind gold-rimmed glasses, Anouilh does not encourage familiarity. "I have no biography, a fact which I find most satisfactory," is the way he answers any personal inquiry. At twenty-three, after the modest success of *The Ermine*, he decided to write plays, nothing but plays, and that is just what he has done—with the exception of an occasional movie script only in order to keep himself alive. He publishes, at a dizzy pace, volumes of plays without "prefaces or confessions": somber "black" plays that end badly; gay

CONTINUED ON PAGE 126

55

A Brilliance in the Bush

Wherever art is a way of life, as it is for the N'debele people of the

Transvaal, beauty can be wrought from the most unlikely materials

"Art is not a pleasure, a solace, or an amusement," Tolstoy said in *What Is Art?* "Art is a matter of prime importance. Art is an organ of human life. . . ." To the N'debele people of South Africa, one of whose colorful villages is the subject of the following portfolio, these are obvious truths which they know without reading Tolstoy—or, for that matter, without reading at all. They live at the subsistence level or below, and they know nothing of the world outside the Transvaal; however, unlike most primitive people who cling to their own ancient ways, they do know something of civilization. Their villages are all within a hundred miles of Pretoria and Johannesburg; their men go to work in the gold fields and their unmarried girls work as house servants, but—so far, at least—virtually all of them come home again. The life of their own villages, with its continual excitement of new building and decorating, is far more satisfying to them than owning a bicycle or a radio in the squalid black townships of Johannesburg. For them, art is an integral and indispensable part of life.

The village shown here, Chief Speelman's village, is about thirty miles outside of Pretoria. In Africa, the outskirts of a city do not spill so far across the landscape as they do in more populated countries; the cities are like islands, and the enormous, lonely countryside comes up close and laps them like a sea. For almost half the way to Chief Speelman's village, the road proceeds past stiffly respectable small houses, filling stations, drive-ins, and used-car lots; take away the signs in Afrikaans, the poinsettias, and the orange trees, and this could be the Middle West or Canada. Then, suddenly, there are no more houses, the paved road ends and turns rough, and the landscape, clear to the horizon, is nothing but gray-brown bush. Then you come over a rise, and there, like a jewel in an ash heap, is the village.

A N'debele village consists of one uneven row of low huts made of clay and cow dung, each hut surrounded by an open courtyard. Left unpainted, they would be lost in the bush; modestly decorated, in the way that a Westerner might think appropriate to their size and proportions, they would be merely insignificant; but as they are, painted in a wonderful show of brilliant color and huge design, they become imposing, the homes of people of consequence. A palace built there in the enveloping bush could hardly achieve a prouder effect or more successfully dominate its surroundings.

All the women of the village are artists, and all the men are craftsmen and connoisseurs. When a man is about to marry, he first builds, next to his own hut, a hut for his prospective bride; or rather he puts up a circular latticework of wooden poles and makes a thatched roof of dried river grass. Then he leaves it to his female relatives to wall in the poles, which is done with a mixture of clay and cow dung painstakingly thrown on in small handfuls until the wooden framework is covered over and safe from termites. A smooth finish is given to the walls by applying wet clay and cow dung with the open hand. As soon as the hut is brought to this stage, the bridegroom pays his *lobola* (usually twelve oxen) and collects his bride. From then on, this hut is the wife's exclusive property. Even children after puberty live in separate huts. The wife's one ambition is to make her surroundings so attractive that her husband will never stray from her. First she builds an open courtyard all around the hut, using mud and cow dung blocks, and divides it into two areas—one in back for household tasks, and one in front for company. Inside the front courtyard she plants a couple of fruit trees and makes a built-in bench all around the walls (the N'debele use no furniture). Next she covers all the hut and courtyard floors with packed-down cow dung, which she polishes in such a way as to give a permanent allover pattern of interesting semicircles.

TEXT CONTINUED ON PAGE 65

By MARY CABLE

A portfolio of photographs by Pete Turner, presented in color gravure, begins on the opposite page with a timeless image of N'debele life: a woman returning from one of her uncounted trips to the well. OVERLEAF: At dawn, only a few chickens are stirring in the brightly painted courtyards of the huts.

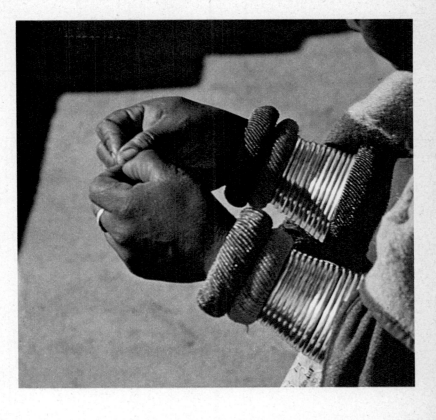

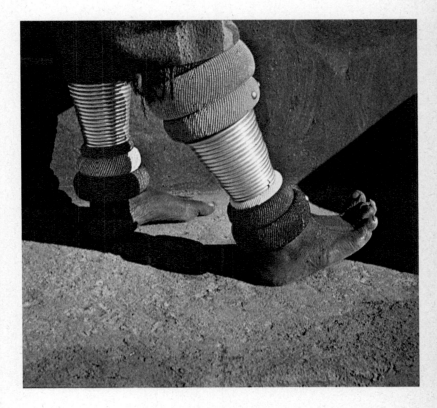

The N'debele woman opposite has ornamented herself with a beaded choker of her own making. Women of the village are also expert at fashioning brass bracelets and anklets, with beadwork adding a contrasting texture.

Life for the women of N'debele village involves the daily pursuit of arts and crafts. Left, a housewife clothed in traditional blanket and jewelry repairs a curb step. Below, another admires the outlines of a new mural before she fills in the colors with an old toothbrush. Opposite, a tribeswoman works on improving the courtyard between strikingly decorated structures—in the foreground, thatched huts painted with geometric designs, and in the rear, a flat-topped house ornamented in a freer, more colorful style.

She is now ready for the major challenge of decorating all the walls. Traditionally, N'debele painting is done in colors obtained from clay deposits in the soil of the Transvaal, and the women have been able to find there every color they want except brilliant blue. White they make from slaked lime and water; black from clay mixed with soot. The colored clay is pulverized and mixed with water to the consistency of putty, and this is moistened further so that it can be applied to the walls with a brush. Near Chief Speelman's village, however, there are no clay deposits—his people were moved by the government to their present site not long ago because the farmer who owned the land where they had lived for generations put them off and burned their village down. The women here have taken to using store paints, which give them the much-prized blue, but for the most part they choose traditional clay colors—with an emphasis on burnt sienna, the commonest color of Transvaal clay—and achieve the effect they want. On the hut front and on the outside front of the courtyard wall, the N'debele wife outlines her own interpretation of a traditional pattern, a pattern whose symbolic meaning has now either been forgotten or is known to the elders of the tribe and kept secret; then she paints it in any color scheme she likes. Brilliant blue is a favorite color, also mustard yellow, coral, and burgundy, all accented with black and white. Side and rear walls are more simply patterned in white and gray or in strokes of white on the rich, brown, clay and dung surface; and this humbler decoration emphasizes the grandeur of the main façades.

A N'debele woman is as much an artist of dress as of décor. She may wear a missionary-inspired cotton bodice and skirt or simply a piece of blanket, but anything she puts on she first encrusts copiously with bright beading, in colors to match the colors of her house. Tubular bead necklaces and bracelets, also in the same color scheme, go around her neck, arms, ankles, and calfs, together with as many homemade brass bangles as she can possibly accommodate. Here again, she shows an artistic sense of proportion: N'debele women are small and slender, and their chokers make them look taller and more dignified. If they wear a great many arm and leg decorations, their shaven heads are left bare or are adorned only with a small beaded band or a pair of hoop earrings. They know when to leave well enough alone.

The bangles and beads are not made to come off at night; washing is said to be accomplished by poking soapy fingers under them. But if necks, arms, and legs are not remarkably clean, huts and courtyards are pristine. The N'debele have scarcely any belongings other than what they are wearing, so there is a minimum of clutter. Bedding, made of a hollow spongy river reed woven into mats, is rolled up when not in use; and the premises are swept and dusted all day long with gorgeously beaded brooms.

The paint wears dim in the rainy season and must be refreshed or, if the owner so fancies, entirely changed. Should a woman die, the hut becomes the property of her children; if she is sent away for unfaithfulness, the hut is turned over to public use—but in no case may another wife inhabit it. Should the husband take a second wife, he prepares a second hut beside the first. If he takes a third wife, and decides that she will be his last, he builds her hut slightly forward of the others, which indicates to the N'debele world that he has retired from the matrimonial field.

The N'debele of the Transvaal are only a remnant of a once great and powerful people. In earlier centuries, this tribe ruled over large areas. By the beginning of the nineteenth century, however, they had already been conquered by the Zulus, but in spite of the Zulu custom of killing all conquered warriors and marrying all conquered women, they managed to retain some tribal identity. During the first half of the nineteenth century, there were revolts in the Zulu nation, and some N'debele fled northward to what later became Rhodesia. When the Boers arrived in the Transvaal, the N'debele they found still remaining there were a peaceful, pastoral people, absorbed, then as now, in the upkeep of elegant villages. They did not share the Zulu zest for waylaying and annihilating parties of Boer pioneers, but they did indulge in cattle lifting. Moreover, their chief, Mapoga (his name was corrupted into "Mapog," and the tribe is still known in the Transvaal as the Mapog people), gave serious annoyance to the Boers by granting sanctuary to a neighboring chief who had a price on his head; and in January, 1883, the Boer leader, General Petrus Joubert, decided to put the Mapogs in their place for good and all.

Mapoga, together with his friend the fugitive chief and some eight thousand tribesmen, took refuge in a region full of caves, and it took General Joubert seven months and a great deal of dynamite to persuade them to surrender. It was an expensive war, considering the insignificance of the Mapogs, and the Boer government decided to prevent them from ever again causing trouble. The whole tribe was split into manageable groups and indentured to farmers in the Pretoria area, many miles from their native home and widely separated from one another. They were to give three months' work a year to the farmer and take care of their own needs the rest of the time. When the indenture period was over, some found that their former lands now belonged to Boer settlers. They stayed where they were and went on working for the farmers and living their own aesthetic life; and so they remain to this day.

Mary Cable is an American writer who now lives in Salisbury, Southern Rhodesia. Her article about The Grand Seraglio *in Istanbul appeared in the May, 1959, issue of* HORIZON.

A sleeping village dog is seen through an opening in a riotously painted wall. Since new motifs are frequently added, the N'debele designs are less static than those employed in most African arts and crafts.

The Archpoet

As a young man, Yeats made old men's verses—he said so himself—but when he grew old, his verse became young

He was a man to whom age gave an extraordinary beauty. Of the poets who have written in this century he was perhaps the greatest, and in his last period he seemed in manner and appearance the archpoet. It was the title his friend Dr. Gogarty rightly gave him, for William Butler Yeats with the years became the ποιητὴς, the poet, not in the restricted literary sense but in the original meaning of the Greek—the maker.

His poetry altered with his appearance, for in his twenties and thirties his verses had the vague opalescence of the Celtic twilight. And so the young Yeats looked, with his Inverness cape, his flowing hair, and flowing tie, as in Sargent's portrait of him. If he had died then, he would have endured only briefly, a felicitous versifier in a minor key, a member of the Rhymers' Club, companion of the Cheshire Cheese, the Irish equivalent of his friends Ernest Dowson and Lionel Johnson. With his wandering Aenguses and lake isles and salley gardens, he would at least have attained the goal he set in "To Ireland in the Coming Times":

> Know, that I would accounted be
> True brother of a company
> That sang, to sweeten Ireland's wrong
>
>   *   *   *   *
>
> Nor may I less be counted one
> With Davis, Mangan, Ferguson, . . .

But he had left those dimmed names in their groves, and his own name was long since secure when he wrote his stoic summing-up in "What Then?":

> His chosen comrades thought at school
> He must grow a famous man;
> He thought the same and lived by rule,
> All his twenties crammed with toil;
> *"What then?" sang Plato's ghost. "What then?"*
>
> Everything he wrote was read,
> After certain years he won
> Sufficient money for his need,
> Friends that have been friends indeed;
> *"What then?" sang Plato's ghost. "What then?"*

> All his happier dreams came true—
> A small old house, wife, daughter, son,
> Grounds where plum and cabbage grew,
> Poets and Wits about him drew;
> *"What then?" sang Plato's ghost. "What then?"*
>
> "The work is done," grown old he thought,
> "According to my boyish plan;
> Let the fools rage, I swerved in naught,
> Something to perfection brought";
> *But louder sang that ghost, "What then?"*

Here was, finally, a man face to face with the ultimate. Yet as the sage developed, so also did the satyr. In Yeats's youth, love was an ideal, and he could write with melodious vagueness:

> All things uncomely and broken, all things
>   worn out and old,
> The cry of a child by the roadway, the creak
>   of a lumbering cart,
> The heavy steps of the ploughman, splashing
>   the wintry mould,
> Are wronging your image that blossoms a rose
>   in the deeps of my heart.

But with age his imagery turned sensual and direct. A wild, wicked old man he would call himself, who regretted the celibacy of his youth and for whom the act of love was now chosen as a "second-best."

> You think it horrible that lust and rage
> Should dance attention upon my old age;
> They were not such a plague when I was
>   young;
> What else have I to spur me into song?

Of the many Yeats portraits—by his father, by Sargent, by Augustus John, by Charles Shannon, and the rest—I think the later one by Mancini was best able to capture his dual nature, the intertwined carnality and nobility.

When William Morris was an Oxford undergraduate and first began to write verses, he wrote almost as readily as he talked. "I do not know whether or not I am a poet," he told his friends, "but it is very easy." Yeats was never gifted with such spontaneity. He

was much more a poet by conscious choice. Ten or a dozen lines a day were his limit, formed, cut, and finally polished. Even so, his finished poems never seemed to him wholly finished. He was a great tinkerer, in after years even going back to reshaping and rewriting his early work.

Yeats was the last of the Homeric succession of poets who wrote more for the ear than the eye, as Arland Ussher remarked, adding that nowadays the eye written for is generally spectacled. But Yeats's poetry, whether the vague verse of his youth or the taut lines of his age, has the singing quality that cannot be defined—it is the music of incantation. The melody that he gave to his lines he evolved by muttering aloud, chanting, singing to himself—"booming and buzzing like a bumble bee," Maud Gonne described him. Even in the delirium of his dying, his lips still formed words.

I met Yeats only once, in the winter of 1932, at Brunswick, Maine, a place and a landscape so alien to Ireland that its incongruity still seems ludicrous. It so happened, however, that Yeats was giving a lecture at Bowdoin where I was at the time an undergraduate.

Isolated though Bowdoin was, many distinguished literary figures came there to lecture, usually staying as guests of President and Mrs. Sills. Mrs. Sills had a celebrated damask tablecloth on which the signatures of such visitors were embroidered. At the formal dinner given before each lecture, all the guests were asked to write their names on the cloth. Later the noteworthy signatures were embroidered in; the rest came out in the wash.

The arrival of such celebrities in a small academic community often created minor practical problems. There was the late Lord Dunsany who, to the mystification of the Sills's general maid, stacked his shoes outside his bedroom door each night. And just before leaving he asked the President's

By FRANCIS RUSSELL

This photograph of Yeats, by Edward Steichen, was made about the time of his Bowdoin lecture in 1932

mother to pack his bag for him. The Irish poet A.E., en route from Portland to Brunswick, managed to get lost in Portland's Grand Trunk Station. When T. S. Eliot arrived to give his lecture on "The Poetry of Lewis Carroll and Edward Lear," although his manners were more considerate, close observers swore that he was wearing a toupee. John Masefield was felt to be the model of all such guests.

No one knew quite what to expect of the Irish archpoet. He had sent word ahead that at the dinner before his lecture no one was to speak to him unless he spoke first. This was not so arrogant as it then seemed, for Yeats suffered at times from incapacitating migraines. As it turned out, he was quite affable and talkative during the dinner.

Afterwards he lectured in the upper auditorium of Memorial Hall, the cavernous Grant-Gothic structure built in imitation of Harvard's even more ferociously Gothic pile memorializing the Civil War dead. Yeats seemed a hierophant of poetry as he appeared on the platform, his aloof head tossed back in what I later learned was a characteristic gesture. The dark hair of his youth, now turned snow-white, was like the stylized lion's mane from some Syrian bas-relief. The modeling of his high nose and chin and somewhat sensuous mouth was stylized, too, but in the manner of the later Greeks. His eyes behind tortoise-shell spectacles—then out of fashion in America, but oddly suited to him—were an oblique, almost Oriental oval. On the little finger of his left hand he wore a ring with a stone so large that it extended from joint to joint. He was the most impressive man I had ever seen. His voice was golden. The recordings of it that remain give no conception of its timbre, the glowing way it filled a room. Oscar Wilde is said to have had such a voice.

Yeats did not read from his own poetry that evening, to the disappointment of his provincial audience—most of whom had come hoping to hear "The Lake Isle of Innisfree," the poem of his youth that he came to detest. He read mostly from James Stephens. I remember my own surprise when he first began with "Deirdre," for he chanted it, swaying slightly, his vibrant voice ritualizing the lines. The effect was impressive, but also—I found—somewhat embarrassing. Anyone but Yeats intoning that way would have made himself ridiculous. I preferred him speaking. His voice then had a hypnotic flow that bore one along with it. He told of once being in Connemara

and giving a coin to an old beggar-woman who thanked him in Gaelic, using a phrase out of Spenser—and as he told us this there was a moment's tremor in his voice to which I responded with a sympathetic tremor.

After the lecture as I walked back across the snow-piled campus to the Mustard House where I roomed, the stars seemed to crackle in the February sky above the bare elm branches. The after-image of that splendid white head still persisted, the unforgettable ringing voice echoed in my mind. Only after I had settled down at my desk did it occur to me that the beggar-woman had spoken in Gaelic, and that Spenser wrote in English!

By the time, ten years later, when I had become a soldier in the Canadian army, Yeats had been dead three years. He died in January, 1939, in Roquebrune in the south of France and was buried in the cemetery above the stone town looking out over the Mediterranean, although he had long wished to be buried in his beloved Sligo under the shadow of the great table mountain. His last weeks and his last strength had been given to revising his epitaph-poem:

> Under bare Ben Bulben's head
> In Drumcliff churchyard Yeats is laid.
> An ancestor was rector there
> Long years ago, a church stands near,
> By the road an ancient cross.
> No marble, no conventional phrase;
> In limestone quarried near the spot
> By his command these words are cut:
>> Cast a cold eye
>> On life, on death.
>> Horseman, pass by!

It had been planned to bring his body back to Ireland in September, but the outbreak of World War II made that impossible.

His posthumous *Last Poems and Plays*, a book of 126 pages that included two one-act plays, appeared in 1940, but I did not get round to ordering a copy until two summers later. One got out of the habit of reading in the army. An officers' training course had delayed my getting overseas, and I was then a two-pip lieutenant in the Canadian infantry training center at Huntingdon, a lonely little loyalist town set down in the middle of rural Quebec. The alien plain enveloped the boxlike wooden houses that seemed to huddle for protection under the enormous arch of the sky. To the north lay the expansion of the St. Lawrence known as Lake St. Francis, and to the south and visible from our parade ground were the last ranges of the Appalachians just across the New York border.

Somehow the crystal succession of summer days encompassed by the routine of drill and training made my prewar world of universities and literary gossip seem trivial. Here was a life stripped of unessentials, sufficient in itself not to need being reflected in books. The isolated camp under the northern sky, the company lines of tar-paper spider huts to which we returned in columns of threes each fading afternoon, these men—myself among them—molded for some remote, unimagined, yet inevitable event across the ocean, formed a basic verity beyond the new, the newer, or the newest criticism. Yeats would have understood, as when he wrote of the scholars:

> Bald heads forgetful of their sins,
> Old, learned, respectable bald heads
> Edit and annotate the lines
> That young men, tossing on their beds,
> Rhymed out in love's despair
> To flatter beauty's ignorant ear.
>
> All shuffle there; all cough in ink;
> All wear the carpet with their shoes;
> All think what other people think;
> All know the man their neighbour knows.
> Lord, what would they say
> Did their Catullus walk that way?

The army could be irrational, at times even sub-rational, but there was in it a bone-bare honesty, something of the quality that Yeats himself found in his old age. One marks the difference between such lush early ballads as "Father Gilligan" and the tautness of the last Parnell or Casement ballads. Somewhere he wrote that when he was a young man he had made old men's verses but when he was old his verse became young. It became not so much young as timeless. Yeats lived a succession of poses —romantic, nationalist, mystic. Even the aloof archpoet was a pose. He liked to think of himself as concealed by a succession of masks, until the mask image became an obsession with him. Yet, at the end, in his noble poem "The Circus Animals' Desertion," he had the courage to drop all his poses, put off all his masks. His themes, his concealments, his pretensions became for him toys—circus animals, he called them—

> Maybe at last, being but a broken man,
> I must be satisfied with my heart, although
> Winter and summer till old age began
> My circus animals were all on show,
> Those stilted boys, that burnished chariot,
> Lion and woman and the Lord knows what.

until finally he was left

> . . . where all the ladders start,
> In the foul rag-and-bone shop of the heart.

Because my life had become almost as stripped as Yeats's in his age, I felt I had only then really understood him. For looked at from the prospect of an army camp, poetry assumes some of its original function before literature absorbed it, as a quickener of life, a consolation in time of trouble. So the *Last Poems* seemed to me as I lay on my upper bunk with my webbing still on but unfastened, in the final quarter of the noon rest hour before the bugle blew, leafing that green volume with a circus animal—in this case a lion—and an Egyptian goddess embossed on the cover. Through the verses I sensed somehow the brooding intensity of our era that at times echoed or seemed to echo the tread of marching feet:

Remember all those renowned generations,
Remember all that have sunk in their blood,
Remember all that have died on the scaffold,
Remember all that have fled, that have stood,
Stood, took death like a tune
On an old tambourine.

The later Yeats was often enigmatic, and I am not sure that even those who knew his personal references could be certain of what he meant at all times, but always there was the extraordinary melody of line that carried one along. Here he dared to ask himself the questions that he had never faced before:

Did that play of mine send out
Certain men the English shot?
Did words of mine put too great strain
On that woman's reeling brain?
Could my spoken words have checked
That whereby a house lay wrecked?

Again, as he showed in his brief poem "Politics," he could transform, without denying, an old man's lust. Finally, near the end of the book, came his one-act play *Purgatory*, in its somber, blood-drenched beauty to my mind his masterpiece. I read only during the noon pause. Living under the shadow of those events across the Atlantic which moved closer with each day, I found myself too restless to spend my evenings in the isolation of a book. As it grew dark I would go with the other officers to the Château, the rickety hotel built as a sanctuary during the American prohibition years and now flourishing for the first time since repeal. The other ranks swarmed downstairs in the beery turbulence of the bull pen. We sat upstairs in the lounge bar that was out of bounds to them. Always our talk, no matter how it began, turned to overseas. Then an hour or so after the bull pen had closed, we wandered back to the now-dark spider huts. The cooling August air was shrill with katy-

Yeats was forty-three when he posed for this portrait in charcoal by John Singer Sargent.

dids, while sometimes beyond Lake St. Francis sheets of northern lights flickered across the horizon. And I would find lines and stanzas of the *Last Poems* running through my head, echoing to my steps. I don't suppose a day passed but I thought of some of them. There were those savage lines in the Ben Bulben poem where the old man, facing his end, parodied the Prayer Book's "Give peace in our time, O Lord," praying for war to make an end to all he hated in our age. Most cruel they were, and yet they had a cold and haunting truth to them.

You that Mitchel's prayer have heard,
"Send war in our time, O Lord!"
Know that when all words are said
And a man is fighting mad,
Something drops from eyes long blind,
He completes his partial mind,
For an instant stands at ease,
Laughs aloud, his heart at peace.
Even the wisest man grows tense
With some sort of violence
Before he can accomplish fate,
Know his work or choose his mate.

Under the shadow, I could not get them out of my mind.

There was one strange poem called "Long-Legged Fly," the first stanza of which haunted me for days:

That civilisation may not sink,
Its great battle lost,
Quiet the dog, tether the pony
To a distant post;
Our master Caesar is in the tent

Where the maps are spread,
His eyes fixed upon nothing,
A hand under his head.
*Like a long-legged fly upon the stream
His mind moves upon silence.*

I don't know what Yeats intended by those lines, whether indeed he intended any modern parallel at all, but to me they became an image of Hitler in his field headquarters as he pored over the maps; the strange, evil, intuitive genius, his mind moving apart from his generals, upon silence. Hitler was the Caesar. So he had appeared, in that tremendous moment of the war's opening, before the Reichstag in a private's field gray. That man, driven by his dark demon, had altered the world more than any man of our age; he had changed, or would change, the lives of every one of us. Through him, I, a continent away, had been plucked from a library and set down as a soldier in this remote Canadian landscape. There were millions like me obscurely wearing khaki, other millions now dying in Eastern Europe to add to the millions already slaughtered, to the populations uprooted and the states and dynasties changed. In that sense he was our master.

Even Yeats himself, in death, did not escape that compelling hand. In spite of the Ben Bulben poem, after the fall of France his body was fated to remain in the Roquebrune cemetery. Not until the autumn of 1948 did the Irish government, with a sense of fitness unusual in modern governments, send the corvette *Macha* to bring him home. At Galway Bay the coffin was piped ashore with naval honors and, from there, taken the ninety miles to Sligo and the Drumcliff churchyard where a military guard was waiting.

It is a question whether Yeats intended his cryptic epitaph for his dead self or whether he saw himself as the rider passing by—or both. There is an equal enigma about his reburial. The coffin exhumed by the Roquebrune sexton was not opened for identification. When it was first seen in the chapel there was no mark of earth on it. The polished wood looked unstained after nine years underground, and the brass fittings glistened. It was carried down the steep rock path to the town square, where it lay in state for a day. There it was seen by many. And there were some who said it did not contain Yeats's body at all.

Francis Russell has written for a wide range of magazines, both American and English, including AMERICAN HERITAGE *and* HORIZON.

A MEMORANDUM

From: H. L. Mencken

To: The President-elect

Subject: On entering the millennium

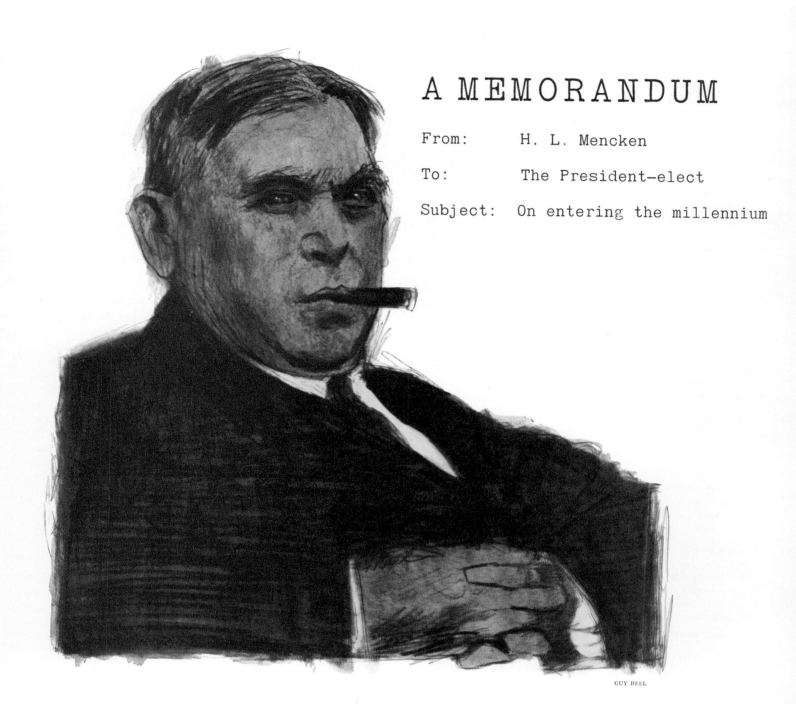

GUY DEEL

Your elders won't believe this, but I rise to offer you a hosanna on your forthcoming succession to the throne of the Republic.

Although you are far too young to recall it, for almost a quarter of a century it was my custom as a student of the higher American mountebankery to cover presidential campaigns at close quarters, from their opening flow of moonshine to the final convulsive sputterings of the rival messiahs on election eve, delivering myself, in the gray light of morning after, of prayers for the laity as to what they were about to receive—which was usually no better than what they deserved.

Like your predecessors, you have assured the body politic that if elected, you will lead it into a Promised Land. But unlike them, I think you have a chance of actually doing so.

In fact, it should not be difficult; for the Great Fulfillment—at home, that is—is already almost here. America is now so changed from the Sahara of the booboisie I knew in my prime that I have the greatest difficulty recognizing it at all. In a relatively short time you seem to have overcome almost all the lags, barbarisms, buffooneries, and downright knaveries that bedeviled my own. With so much progress already achieved, I shall wager a McKinley double eagle and a case of Schloss Johannisberg 1929 that you now stand on the verge of a Gilead of general enlightenment.

The great oppressions of my own day have been lifted. You have long since banished Prohibition, save in a few backwaters deep in the chiggers belt, and New York City's proudest new architectural monument is the temple of a distilling company. You have put down the scourges of Puritan-

By WILLIAM HARLAN HALE

ism and censorship: today everything goes in print or on stage and screen—and woe betide the author who doesn't put in all the facts of life or the Post Office that ventures to take them out. There are hardly any Babbitts or Coolidges still at large, either: the lodge-joiners and Rotary sooth-sayers of my time have since become farsighted industrial statesmen, cultivating their workers with picture windows and piped-in Bizet, and even the stoneheads of innermost Vermont now support aid to farthest Nepal.

You are not only more adult than we were, but you agree so much more. Your politicos, for instance, no longer go through the old annual dumb-show of rivaling each other with promises to reduce the budget without having the slight-est intention of doing anything of the sort; today there's honest understanding all around that the only thing to do with budgets is to increase them. Most of your highest oracles have also wisely abandoned the old custom of writ-ing or trying to write their own speeches, thus sparing the Republic much ungrammatical bilge-water; their dithy-rambs are now composed for them, I understand, chiefly by *Time* and *Life* editors, Harvard professors, and Madison Avenue thinkers-in-residence, with results that are at least smooth, although interchangeable. In fact, so smoothly has everything gone in this new day—on our own home ground, at least—that you now have virtually interchangeable parties and candidates, too; and until the mishap of that flying ma-chine over darkest Russia in the spring, it looked as if you might even have a campaign without an issue.

Although that electoral contest is raging while I compose this, I sense that its brickbats are being hurled chiefly in observance of a rite, and that America has no real villains any more. Nor does it have more than a dwindling handful of genuine freaks, grotesques, and anthropoid holdovers. Gone are the Anti-Saloon League, the Methodist Board of Temperance, Prohibition, and Public Morals, the revivalist dervishes and fundamentalist mullahs who once convulsed yokelry. Where are the wowsers and witch doctors I once knew so well, along with the gaping primates who came out of their Appalachian caves to applaud the Scopes trial? You have no Tom Heflins, no Aimee Semple McPhersons, no pri-mordial Dr. John Roach Straton policing your literature, no windjammer like the late Dr. Harding impersonating the ship of state, no backleg camorra like the Ohio gang overtly making off with your money.

And this, while I say *"Prosit!"* does give me pause for some second thoughts. With the decline of low comedy and blatant buncombe, may not a certain spice go out of American life? What, amid so much betterment, *do* you have to enliven the scene and keep the intelligent in arms?

You seem to have no true mavericks and loners, either. Don't give me your beatniks: they have done so well for themselves with their collective mummery that they have

moved into the higher income brackets as the kept lunatic-fringe of the Establishment. I almost think that America has swallowed up its opposition. You now have a nation in which reformed Drys tipple on expense account; in which writers who in my day would have been hounded by the Watch & Ward Society are crowned by the American Academy of Arts and Letters; in which antivivisectionists, Single Taxers, and ex-wobblies now read the *Wall Street Journal* and the *Ever-green Review* beside their free-form swimming pools, while chiropractors, morticians, and Knights of Pythias share a passion for hi-fi sets, Vivaldi, and modern jazz with Insti-tute of Advanced Study *philosophes* and the higher clergy; a country in which, finally, there are few critics, because there appears so little left to criticize.

You have the opportunity, Mr. President, of leading an increasingly literate, prosperous, and worldly people into an Elysium of the most advanced unanimity. And if there are any remaining questions about our National Purpose, these, as you know, have been referred to nonpartisan presidential committees, foundation study groups, mass-magazine pan-els, and task forces of eminent Chevrolet dealers, all bent on ironing out any possible differences. There will be massed Excelsior banners and a prevalent strumming of harps. I only ask myself, isn't this going to get a trifle dull? What's paradise without an occasional horselaugh?

In the raw, backward America in which I was reared, we could always count on a certain number of self-propelled dissenters, jokers, cranks, literary *anarquistas*, and other rude and engaging fellows. Indeed, a quizzical, irreverent, I'm-from-Missouri streak in many of its citizens was one of the nation's saving graces then. But who's to heave dead cats into sanctuaries now, if the opposition's gone—or has be-come part of the sanctuary itself?

What America has achieved today goes so far beyond any-thing I myself had dreamed of that I now begin to wonder whether something shouldn't be done to slow the process before it gets out of hand. If opposition's obsolete, hadn't you better go about creating one yourself, simply in your own interest? Before the forums, foundations, and commit-teemen achieve their goal of total agreement, hadn't you better set up a countercommittee, bureau, or independent executive agency of your own—a Commission for the Ad-vancement of Nonconformity, say?

Do I hear objections to this on the ground that the gov-ernment should not subsidize quixotic causes? Then look at all those it already does subsidize. No one could deplore any more than I any further extension of government activity, with the multiplication of tithe-takers, drones, and boob-squeezers this is likely to entail. But someone has got to make our millennium livable; and if the electorate on its own won't do so, the man to revive its critical spirit, I fear, may have to be you.

NAVIGATOR
to the
MODERN AGE

The crusading and scientific ardor of a medieval prince, Henry of Portugal, drove his sailors across uncharted seas—and brought Europe a new picture of the world, followed by five centuries' dominion over it

Five hundred years ago there died in a storm-battered little castle, perched on a cliff at the extreme southwestern corner of Europe, a medieval prince who was the father of the modern world. We have come to call him "Henry the Navigator," although he never sailed farther than the coast of Morocco just across from Portugal, and probably never navigated anything. He gave his father's house and the cheerful, comfortable, slightly backward little nation his father ruled, one of the most far-flung empires and one of the richest overseas trades the world had ever seen; but no progeny of his succeeded to that empire, and it seems doubtful whether trade or empire had much place in his plans. We can only guess at what those plans were, and what forces drove him to change the whole picture of the world.

We find him baffling, inscrutable. So did his contemporaries. The face which looks out from the "panel of Prince Henry" in the famous reredos at Lisbon is different from all the surrounding faces, not just because it is swarthier, not because the eyes are more brooding and the forehead more lined with thought, but because the whole countenance is marked

The aloof, brooding aspect of Henry's nature marks this portrait, one of two made during his life. This page from a Portuguese chronicle bears his motto, "The gift for doing good."

by a deliberate stillness; withdrawn, aloof, it looks as if no one else existed, as if there was nothing at all except the vision or puzzle on which his attentive eyes are fixed. All we can be sure of is that he is seeing something no one else can see.

What it was he saw, he never said. His was a voluble, mercurial, self-dramatizing family, given to noisy quarrels and tearful reconciliations, to violence and rhetoric (after all, he and his brothers were half Plantagenets), to childishly magnificent display and childishly cunning political charades. Amidst all this uproar, Prince Henry moved like an abstracted adult through the noisy play of children. Even his generosity had something absent-minded about it, so that while men respected him and served him gladly, it seems unlikely that many loved him. His family was literate, even literary, and for men of their time, unusually self-explanatory, but Henry wrote nothing, except perhaps a few prayers, that was not strictly utilitarian. His letters, for the most part, are as dry and businesslike as if he were the bailiff of his own estates. Nowhere is there a line to tell us what he hoped and dreamed. The clues to that are in what happened.

What happened began like a tale in a romance of chivalry. The three eldest sons of King John I of Portugal—Duarte, Pedro, and Henrique (Edward, Peter, and Henry)—had grown up during an uneasy truce with Castile which only the

73

By GARRETT MATTINGLY

year before had been converted into a permanent peace. Now, in 1411, they were, respectively, twenty, nineteen, and seventeen, and it was high time they should be knighted. But there was no enemy against whom they might win their spurs; so their father planned a series of magnificent tournaments to which all the best knights of Europe would be invited and where the three princes might exhibit their prowess at the risk of nothing more than a few bumps and bruises. The king had no more than begun his plans when his sons sought an audience and knelt at his feet. Let not the wealth of the kingdom, they implored, be squandered on vain displays and mock battles. Let them, instead, flesh their swords on the enemies of Portugal and of the Christian faith. Portugal had been born of the Crusade. With their new dynasty, let the Crusade begin again. And since the lands of Castile lay athwart the way to the nearest infidels, the Moors of Granada, let them requite the old insults of past invasions and strike at the paynims, this time on their own African soil. Let them attempt the conquest of Ceuta.

It was a surprising suggestion. People still talked about the Crusade but seldom did anything about it. Crusading had gone out of fashion. The princes' uncle, Henry IV of England, said often enough that he hoped one day to lead an army to liberate the Holy Land and lay his bones at last somewhere near the sepulcher of his Saviour, but the nearest he got to doing so was to die amidst his ill-gotten gains in the Jerusalem Chamber at Westminster. As for his son, the future Henry V, he found a nearer and richer enemy more attractive, and would soon be setting out to demonstrate his superior claim to the crown of France by burning the wretched villages of his prospective subjects. In general, throughout Europe, Christian princes preferred to pursue their vendettas with one another while they wrangled over which of the three current popes best deserved their allegiance. Christendom seemed to be shrinking and breaking up. The Ottoman Turks, quickly recovering from the awful blow dealt them by Tamerlane, pressed forward again on its eastern flank. Even in Portugal, which from one end to the other had been carved out of Moslem territory by the swords of crusaders, nobody had done any serious crusading for a hundred and fifty years.

Nevertheless, when he came to think of it, King John could see merits in his sons' suggestion. Ceuta, lying just across the straits from Gibraltar, was the chief port of the Barbary corsairs. It could watch all the shipping that went to and fro in the strait. From Ceuta swooped the swift galleys to seize Italian merchantmen making for Lisbon or to raid the little villages of the Portuguese Algarve and carry off men, women, and children to the slave markets of Africa. Moreover, Ceuta was the favorite staging area and jumping-off-place for the hordes of desert fanatics who from time to time had swept into Spain. To hold it was to hold one of the chief keys to the whole peninsula. Finally, Ceuta was the chief terminus west of Algiers for the caravan trails which came up across the great desert from the wealthy Negro kingdoms of the south. The bazaars and warehouses would be stuffed with monkeys and parakeets, ostrich plumes and elephants' tusks, rare woods and Guinea pepper, and there would be leather bags of gold dust and wedges of reddish-yellow gold tucked away in the strong rooms of every prosperous merchant. At the very least there would be rich spoil, and if the caravans would keep coming, the trade of Africa might fill the coffers of Portugal. When his spies reported that Ceuta might prove vulnerable to determined assault, King John began to make his preparations.

There was a great deal to do. Portugal had to buy cannon and gunpowder abroad, and even ordinary arms and armor. It had to hire ships. And it was impossible in a poor little kingdom to keep these expensive preparations secret; so all of Portugal's neighbors got justifiably nervous. There was grave danger that Castile might take alarm and, thinking these preparations were meant against her, strike first. There was even graver danger that Ceuta might smell the threat and strengthen her defenses. A properly prepared Ceuta would be, against any possible Portuguese effort, impregnable. But by an elaborate comedy of misdirection, King John actually succeeded in persuading observers that what he was preparing was an invasion of—of all places—Holland, so that when the Portuguese armada turned south from Lisbon, the watchful Moors were astonished and dismayed. Even though a tempest blew the invasion fleet off station before a surprise attack could be mounted, Moorish vigilance and Moorish valor could not stop the wild rush of the Portuguese who came boiling off their little ships and splashing through the shallows with Prince Henry at their head. There was savage fighting in the narrow, twisty streets, but before nightfall the last Moorish defenders had fled, and King John was able to knight his three sons in the first city, outside Europe, taken from the infidels in almost three hundred years.

The loot of Ceuta was richer even than had been anticipated. This was a city as stuffed with treasure as Venice, and though most of the gold and precious stones seem to have vanished into the pockets of seamen and archers and men-at-arms, the immediate profit to the crown made the venture a success. But for the long pull, Ceuta was a liability. No more caravans brought the wealth of Ghana across the Sahara to its bazaars. No more merchants from Cairo came with the silks and spices of the East. The wooded hills behind Ceuta were full of Moorish partisans, and the place was under vir-

On the rocky, wind-swept promontory of Sagres *(above)* at the southwest tip of Europe, where today a fortress stands in ruins, Henry lived and established his renowned scientific academy. There he brought about improvements in navigation, map-making, and shipbuilding. His captains first sailed in the clumsy barca *(right, on a 15th-century faïence bowl)* but later used the graceful caravel *(below, from the "Miller Atlas" of 1519 by Lopo Homem).*

One object of Henry's probes along the African coast was to make contact, hopefully via a "Western Nile," with the legendary Christian ruler Prester John. His fabled kingdom lay somewhere beyond the Moors, perhaps in Ethiopia, where Diogo Homem pictured him, enthroned as above, on a map of 1558.

tual siege except when its former ruler found enough allies to make the siege close and actual. In either case, a strong Portuguese garrison had to be maintained, and the whole town, Christians and Moors alike, had to be fed by sea by convoys escorted by war galleys. For a little country like Portugal, the drain of such an outpost was heavy and the advantage doubtful. No one expected in 1415, when the eyes of Europe were fixed on Agincourt and Constance and on all the internal squabbles which were weakening Christendom against the advancing Turk, that the capture of Ceuta marked the reversal of a trend and that, henceforward, instead of contracting, as it had done for the past two hundred years, Europe would begin to expand again until its civilization circled and dominated and began to unite the globe. It was for no such reason that the Portuguese hung on to Ceuta; they did so simply because it seemed shameful to abandon a city won from the infidels.

The burden of its defense was laid on Prince Henry. Some months after the taking of the city, when he was only twenty-two, his father appointed him Governor of Ceuta and, a little later, Lieutenant-General of the Kingdom of the Algarve, the southernmost province of Portugal, and Grand Master of the crusading Order of Christ. Entrusting the actual command of the garrison at Ceuta to a deputy, the prince himself undertook the harder task of maintaining the line of supply. At first he lived mostly near the sleepy little port of Lagos on the south coast. Later he spent more and more time on the wind-swept headlands of Cape St. Vincent looking out south and west over the tumbling Atlantic. And

sometime in those years he saw the vision and accepted the mission to which, with monklike dedication, he devoted the rest of his life. In an ominous waxing crescent, the great world of Islam, stretching from the Russian steppes to the Atlantic coast of Morocco, hemmed in and threatened the smaller Christian world. But beyond the barrier of Islam to the east and south were non-Islamic peoples, some of them (nobody knew how many) Christians. If Islam could be outflanked, the old enemy could be taken in the rear and the Crusade resumed. There was only one way to do it—by sea.

The thing to do was to sail south down the African coast. Henry's earliest chronicler, Zurara, sets forth the prince's objectives as if they had been analyzed by a staff for a command decision. The date, he implies, was about 1419, when Henry was first setting up his court at Sagres. A scientific objective: to explore the coast of Africa beyond the Canary Islands and Cape Bojador because at that time nothing was known by experience, or from the memories of men, or from books, of the land beyond that cape. An economic objective: to seek beyond the cape countries with whom it would be possible to trade. A military objective: to find out by reconnaissance how far south the country of the Moors extended, since a prudent man tries to learn the strength of his enemy. A political objective: to seek a Christian kingdom as an ally. A religious objective: to extend the faith. More than thirty years later, Duarte Pacheco told a somewhat different story. "One night," he said, "as the Prince lay in bed it was revealed to him that he would render a great service to our Lord by the discovery of the Ethiopians . . . that many of them could be saved by baptism . . . and that in their lands so much gold and other riches would be found as would maintain the king and people of Portugal in plenty and enable them to wage war on the enemies of our holy Catholic Faith." There is at least a poetic truth in Pacheco's version, for what turned out to be the greatest series of scientific experiments ever conducted up to that time by Western man, a series which changed the face of the globe and introduced the modern age, began in the haze of a medieval dream. The dream is explicit in the fourth of Zurara's dryly stated objectives: to seek a Christian kingdom as an ally. That could only be the kingdom of Prester John.

Probably the first Prester John heard of in Europe was some Turkish chieftain of the Eastern steppes, some sort of Buddhist or, perhaps, Nestorian Christian, a priest and king at enmity with neighboring Moslems. Later, Prester John became identified with the Coptic Christian overlord of the Abyssinian highland, some of whose priests had chapels at Jerusalem and Bethlehem and some of whose envoys, or persons representing themselves as his envoys, occasionally found their way to Rome and the courts of the West. Medieval Europe was able to transfer the same king, with the same legend, from central Asia to northeast Africa with a minimum of trouble, for both lands lay "somewhere toward the Indies" on the borders of myth and fable. Here unicorns strayed and griffins guarded gold. Here were cannibals, and men whose heads did grow beneath their shoulders, and other men who hopped about on one leg with an enormous foot which, when they took a noonday siesta, they used as an umbrella. Here was a nation of giants who hunted dragons, using lions as hunting dogs. In the midst of these wonders, Prester John dwelt in a high-perched impregnable castle, its moat a constantly flowing river, not of water but of precious stones, and in its throne room a magic mirror in which the Priest King could see at will any part of the world. Seven kings served at his court, sixty dukes, and three hundred and sixty counts. Seventy-two kings obeyed him. Thousands of war elephants marched at his command and hundreds of thousands of horsemen, to say nothing of a special division mounted on ostriches and another on camelopards. His foot soldiers were as innumerable as the sands of the sea. The legends of Prester John vary. In one he was John, the Beloved Disciple, who could not die before the Second Coming and so sat, meditating on his mountain, guarded by hosts of the faithful, awaiting the day of the Last Judgment. But however the legends vary, there is one common factor: in all, the Priest King is very wealthy and very powerful, a reputation which, one may be sure, such subjects of the Ethiopian emperor as reached the West did nothing to diminish. To reconnoiter the Moorish left flank, and perhaps to divert to Portugal the trade which the Moors had diverted from Ceuta, to increase knowledge and convert the heathen, these were all worthy objectives, but the grand objective was

to find Prester John and reunite the broken halves of Christendom in a renewal of the Crusade.

The only way to get in touch with Prester John was by sea. And by sea there were, geographically, two possibilities. Either Africa was a peninsula, almost an island, or it was not. Herodotus said it was and that a bold crew of Punic seamen had once sailed down its west coast and emerged, after three years, at the head of the Red Sea. Nobody was known to have repeated their feat since, and certainly not all of Herodotus's geographical information was thoroughly reliable; but some Greek, some Arabic, and some Western geographers spoke of Africa as a peninsula, though they differed about how far it might extend to the south. The contrary opinion, however, was sustained by the great authority of Ptolemy, an authority never greater than in the first years of Prince Henry's mission, for the first complete Latin translation of Ptolemy's geography had just been published in 1410. Ptolemy was sure that the land masses north and south of the equator must be roughly equal, otherwise the globe would be overbalanced. So the great world map constructed from his gazetteer shows Africa curving round until it joins with Asia, making the Indian Ocean a vaster Mediterranean.

Nevertheless, Prince Henry thought the best chance of reaching Prester John was to sail south past Cape Bojador. For even if Ptolemy were right, and the way by sea was blocked, there might be another way to the fabled kingdom. Some Arab sages said that the Nile which flowed through Egypt rose in a great lake amidst the Mountains of the Moon. And out of that same lake, they said, flowed another mighty river, the Western Nile, which took its course through the land of the Negroes and emptied into the Atlantic. At least one fourteenth-century map showed both rivers with, right between them and near the shores of the lake in the Mountains of the Moon, the magic castle of Prester John. Now it was well known that through wealthy Ghana flowed a great river (the Niger, really) with rich cities on its banks. It was not unreasonable to assume that the kings of these cities, like the Ethiopians farther east, were the subjects and vassals of the Priest King, and that the ascent of their River of Gold might lead directly to the Priest King's court. So Prince Henry said to his captains, "Go south!"

Nevertheless, for fourteen years none of them got south of Cape Bojador. Their resources were somewhat limited.

Most years, there were at sea in the prince's service not more than two or three *barcas*, the kind of ships the Portuguese used in fishing for tunny or hauling wine and grain along the coast—half-decked vessels shaped like butter tubs with one stubby mast and one clumsy great square sail amidships, commanded by daring, impecunious fidalgos and manned by fishermen from the neighborhood of Lagos. They were not afraid of blue water, however, and they knocked about a good deal in the Atlantic, perhaps looking for the islands, real or imaginary, with which all medieval maps dotted the Ocean Sea, perhaps testing Ptolemy's hypothesis that India was, after all, not very far west of Spain. In the course of their voyages they touched the Canaries and discovered, or rediscovered, the Madeiras and the Azores. And every year one or more of them went down to Cape Bojador, took a good look, and came away again. In spite of Prince Henry's repeated exhortations to go farther south, that was as far as any of them went.

It is not that it is so hard to round Cape Bojador. It's an insignificant little bump on the coast of Africa, and once you have reached it, the difficulty is *not* to round it. Most of the time a wind blows steadily from the northeast—the wind Yankee sailors called, hundreds of years later, "the Portygee Trades"—a wind capable of shoving even a tubby Portuguese *barca* along at a stiff clip while the current tugs at her keel with a force of another knot and a half. But out to seaward, as far as the eye can see, there is brown shoal water with here and there a tumble of breakers. Once past this cape, with no sea room to maneuver and the wind and current against you, how would you ever get back? Rounding Cape Bojador was like entering the mouth of a trap. That is what men were convinced it was, a death trap, for the wind and current would be thrusting you on into the Green Sea of Darkness.

The legend of the Green Sea of Darkness begins with the theories of the Greek geographers. Basically, they said, the globe was divided into five zones. At either pole there was a

Frigid Zone, where men could not live because it was too cold. Its outer ring was merely inhospitable, gradually becoming incapable of supporting life. Nearer the pole, the air was so mixed with frozen water that it was opaque and unbreathable. One Greek traveler actually claimed to have seen this interesting phenomenon. Then there was the Temperate Zone, with the best climate, of course, in Greece, getting gradually too hot in Egypt and too cold in Scythia. In the Southern Hemisphere there was another Temperate Zone, the Antipodes, where, some said, everything in the north Temperate Zone was exactly reproduced. But it would be impossible to find out because between the two lay the Torrid Zone. In it the heat of the sun grew so fierce that no man could hope to cross the Torrid Zone and live.

To this symmetrical Greek picture, the Arabs added horrors of their own to describe the sea beyond Cape Bojador. As the sun grew hotter, the steaming sea became a thickening broth coated with a scum of green weed and infested with loathsome monsters. Near the equator the sea boiled, the tar would boil in a ship's seams, and the brains would boil in a man's skull. But it was unlikely that any ship could get that far. Long before, it would have been dragged to the bottom by the huge sea serpents which abounded in the region, or crunched up like a biscuit by a crocodile bigger than the biggest whale. Allah had placed the Green Sea for a barrier across the southern ocean. Even to attempt to enter it was blasphemy.

Only the most ignorant believed that the world was flat and that men who sailed too far would fall off the edge, but geographers, Arab and Latin, took the Green Sea of Darkness seriously. Nobody knew just where it began, and many must have rejected its more spectacular terrors, but there was considerable agreement that the ocean south of Cape Bojador was dangerous. At least no one had sailed it and returned. In 1291 two Genoese brothers had rounded Bojador, making for India by sea. They were never heard of again. Half a century later, an adventurous Catalan expedi-

TEXT CONTINUED ON PAGE 83

Before the time of Prince Henry, the northwest coast of Africa, seen here on a chart of 1468 by the Venetian Grazioso Benincasa, was known only from Gibraltar (upper right) to Cape Bojador ("Cauo de buçedor," opposite the brightly colored Canary Islands). Beyond were the imagined terrors of the Green Sea of Darkness. In 1434 one of Henry's captains ventured past Bojador and returned safely, and within a few years the Portuguese had sailed 400 miles farther south to Cape Blanco (bottom). The intersecting rhumb lines show wind directions.
OVERLEAF: The dramatic results of Portuguese exploration during the remainder of Henry's century are recorded on the splendid Cantino Planisphere of 1502, most of which is reproduced on the following two pages. En route to distant India (far right) Portugal's seafarers had rounded Africa—whose coast is drawn with remarkable accuracy, while the unexplored interior is rich in medieval fancy—and had touched Brazil and noted her parrots (lower left). The heavy vertical line at the left, fixed by an agreement of 1494, distinguishes Portuguese holdings in the New World (east of the line) from those of Spain. Note that Labrador and Greenland (top), recently rediscovered by Portugal, have been placed too far to the east by the Lisbon cartographer, who clearly wanted to strengthen his country's claim to lands near the demarcation line.

78

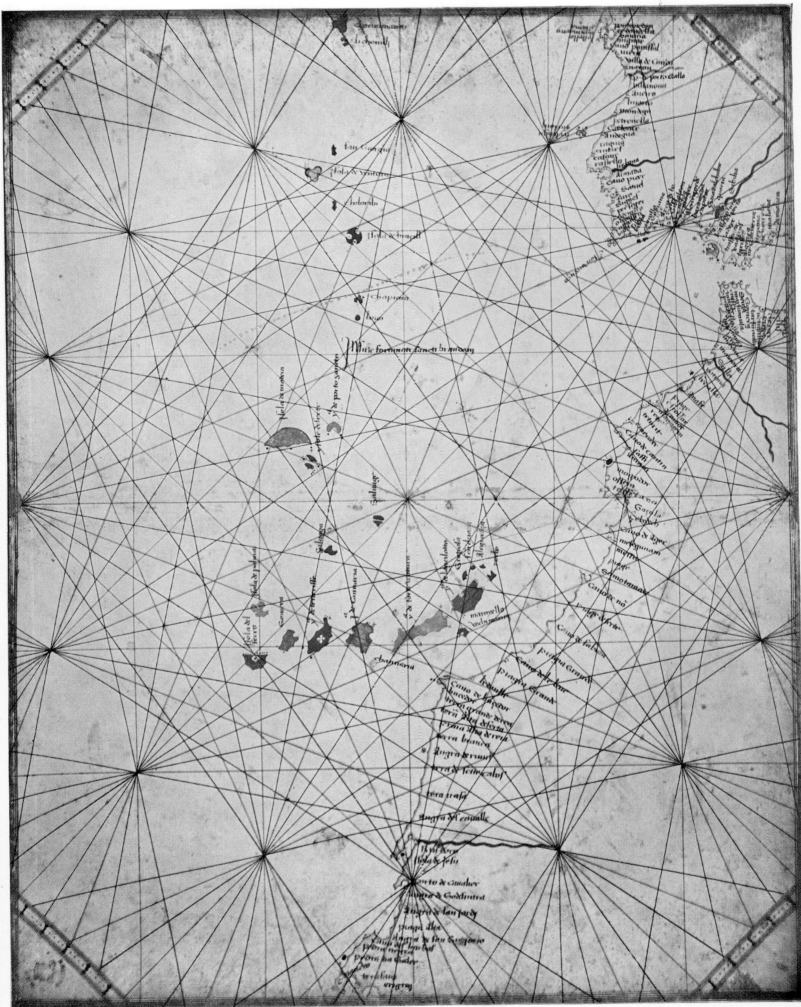

Circulus articus.

Terra del Rey de portuguall

Mar germanice

s del Rey de castella

Esta he o mar sanctar castella e portuguall

Os montes

Lixboa

niara del Rey de castella

Ylinha equinociaalis.

Mare occeanus.

Pollus antarticus.

tion on the same course, looking this time for the River of Gold (the Western Nile?), also disappeared without a trace. Understandably, even brave Portuguese fidalgos hung back. But Prince Henry still said, "Go farther south."

Then, in 1434, after these probes into the vast spaces of the ocean had gone on for fourteen years, one of the prince's captains, Gil Eannes, rounded Cape Bojador and returned. The sea and the wind and the sandy desert shore seemed much the same on one side of the cape as on the other, and the next year Eannes went farther, and the next year one of his companions went farther still, four hundred miles into an unexplored ocean along an unexplored coast. Then came a pause. A disastrous campaign in Morocco and serious domestic disorders distracted Henry's attention, and without the prince's driving will nobody went exploring.

In that interval a great step forward must have been taken in the development of the vessel which made possible the conquest of the ocean. According to Zurara, Gil Eannes rounded Bojador in a *barca*. Nobody says what ships made the next two voyages, and no record survives of how the new type was developed; but when exploration was resumed in 1441, only caravels were used, caravels built in Prince Henry's port of Lagos, expressly, one assumes, for the prince's captains. Caravels continued to carry the explorers until almost the end of the century. They were longer, narrower, more graceful ships than *barcas,* with lateen sails—the primitive form of the fore and aft rig—on two or three masts. They could lie close to the wind and were capital for inshore work. "The best ships in the world and able to sail anywhere," wrote the Venetian Cadamosto after he had commanded one for Prince Henry. For some years, only the Portuguese built caravels, and they sedulously cultivated the legend that no other type of ship could make the African voyage.

We know nothing, except by inference, of Prince Henry's role in the development of the caravel. And we know almost as little of the famous "school" which he set up at his villa at Sagres. He early drew there Jaime of Majorca, prince of cartographers and instrument makers, a man learned in everything that concerned the stars and the sea, the son of the great Abraham Cresques who designed the Catalan Atlas, and possessor, probably, of his father's books and maps. But Henry was always drawing learned men to Sagres, and experienced pilots and far-wandering travelers. It was not so much a school, really, as a sort of scientific congress in con-

tinuous session, working out for the first time the problems of navigating the trackless ocean and of charting unknown coasts by using what the northerners knew of tides and the lead line, what the Italians knew of stars and compass piloting, what could be learned from the Arabs, and what from the ancient Greeks—all to be tested by continuous experiment at sea.

Henry died in 1460, just as his captains began reporting that the African coast was trending to the east. He must have died hoping that Prester John and the fabulous Indies were now not far off. They were more than a generation off, actually, but the back of the problem was broken. By compass and quadrant, Portuguese pilots were finding their way across the trackless ocean, standing boldly out from the Cape Verdes to make a landfall at the Azores, harnessing the great wind systems of the Atlantic—the trades and the westerlies—confidently to their purpose. The African coast was mapped as far as the beginning of the Gulf of Guinea. So were the islands. And sugar from Madeira and cargoes of slaves from Negroland were helping to finance the exploring voyages. Men had seen a new heaven and a new earth, the lush green land beyond the Sahara and the rising constellations of the Southern Hemisphere. And, best of all, the superstitious terrors of the Sea of Darkness, the scientific terrors of the Torrid Zone had been dispersed forever. The ocean south of Cape Bojador was like the ocean north of it. There were no clinging weeds, no horrendous monsters, and a man on the deck of a ship off Sierra Leone, less than ten degrees from the equator, was no more uncomfortably hot than he might have been on a July day in the streets of Lagos. To the south, anyway, there were no unnavigable seas, no uninhabitable lands.

More than forty years of patient, probing experiment had at last made Europeans free of the ocean. From this the voyages of Vasco da Gama and Columbus and Magellan, the European settlement of the Americas, the European commercial dominance of Asia and Africa necessarily followed, and with these things followed too the revolutions, in men's ways of thinking and of making a living, which ended the Middle Ages. The monkish ardor of a medieval prince, his long quest for a mythical kingdom, made inevitable the modern world.

Garrett Mattingly, author of The Armada *and* Catherine of Aragon, *is professor of European history at Columbia.*

The discovery of new lands soon inspired a golden age of cartography. This page from Guillaume le Testu's atlas of 1555 shows the African coast from the Gulf of Guinea, which Henry's caravels were nearing when he died in 1460, south to the Cape of Good Hope, circled by Dias in 1487. Trade in gold, ivory, and slaves made the Guinea coast of great value to Portugal; forts were built there to prevent Spanish incursions. Represented beneath a crescent flag is the semibarbaric Christian Kingdom of Congo, founded by ambassadors from Lisbon; on the blue banners are Portuguese arms. Natives resembling classic Greeks are seen fighting, while at sea Neptune rides northward on a fantastic dolphin, his chariot adorned with heraldic emblems of the French admiral, Gaspar de Coligny, to whom le Testu dedicated the atlas.

On Stage: RONNY GRAHAM

Ronny Graham, one of the few people in show business equipped to put on full make-up merely by not shaving between noon and ten o'clock at night, is a comedian, composer, lyricist, night-club-revue *feuilletoniste*, and piano player so whimsically bolted together as to give the impression of having been wrought in two sections, each plainly intended for someone else. While most of him is tall, thin, and reasonable, the rest, perched perilously between his shoulders like a tourist on a camel, is broad, splayed, and eccentric. In fact, Graham's mouth is wide enough to house sixty-four teeth and seems to. His remaining features, set about at random on the order of the late Bull Montana's, are equally generous, so that what might be no more than a look of, say, mild disbelief or simple longing on another man's face turns out to be cosmic incredulity or wild rapacity on Graham's. His voice has the resonance of a moosecall. His eyes are brown, perfectly round, and have obviously never been closed.

This is a fine Gothic façade behind which to operate. There is abundant evidence that Graham's mind is as richly carved as his exterior and is appropriately severe in its concern for the spiritual welfare of his parishioners, a dedicated lot, of whom it may be said that they come to pray and remain to laugh. Like a number of his physically less remarkable contemporaries—Mort Sahl, Lenny Bruce, and Shelley Berman, for example—Graham is dismayed at the state of the world. His attack, however, is more oblique—almost his only excursion into direct political commentary was a sketch presented some years ago in which he had Congressman J. Parnell Thomas accuse Santa Claus of being a Red—and he prefers instead to set fire to large areas of common acceptance.

Thus, one of Graham's sardonic reflections on popular sentiment may be discerned in his "Glenn Ford March," which reads stirringly:

> *Glenn Ford, you're adored*
> *Ever since you appeared in "Gilda";*
> *Glenn Ford, you're adored*
> *More than Lee J. Cobb or Brandon de Wilde.*
> *May your ship of prosperity never sink.*
> *I love you with all my might,*
> *But I still reserve the right*
> *To say to you, Glenn Ford—you stink!*

Two of the characters indissolubly associated with the performer who created them are a literary fellow named Truman Kaput (whom Graham introduced in the well-remembered *New Faces of 1952*, a Broadway exhibit he more or less surrounded as chief clown, lyricist, and sketch writer) and a wondrously deranged pianist known as the bop professor. The latter, first presented by Graham at the now-defunct *boîte*, the Ruban Bleu, is an affectionate tribute to the berserk cabaret performer Harry (The Hipster) Gibson.

Although Graham's disciples along the café circuits are eager to observe the creations of the peripatetic clown, they are currently more often exposed to his harangues as delivered by other performers, for Graham is sought after as a writer of songs and sketches (he has just written the lyrics for a Broadway musical based on Howard Shaw's droll book *The Crime of Giovanni Venturi*). Those eager to hear the master delivering his own material, however, may consult two long-playing records as frequently as their sanity permits.

Graham is, of course, an organic whole, but with a little shaking it is possible to sift out the elements that comprise the total artist. Technically, the last two words of the "Glenn Ford March" are directly traceable to an early taste for surprise and perversity: as a child in a Philadelphia grammar school, Graham wrote a poem on safety for an automobile-club house organ and was denied publication for refusing to make its last line rhyme. From his mother, a former vaudevillian, he acquired a feeling for the grotesque: she was fond of reading to her children particularly graphic newspaper accounts of murders, and she rid herself of a maid by appearing, gibbering, in the girl's bedroom late one night with a bed sheet over her head. From Robert Benchley he drew a sense of narration and demonstration; from Dwight Fiske, an appreciation of rhythmic musical construction (like Fiske, Graham sometimes accompanies himself at the piano); and from Danny Kaye, an affinity for pure nonsense, for logical sound firmly laid over meaninglessness.

His social conscience is his surrealist own. "I don't see being just a hunk of the community," he said not long ago. "I don't mean to kill yourself is a good thing, either. If I'd made a certain kind of surrender, I think I could have been, maybe, in terms of bovine happiness, happier than I am now. But what are you trying to save? Your good name? Keep saving it, it won't mean anything, anyway. Conserve yourself at all costs and you'll be dead, and you won't know it." He ran a hand through his hair. "I don't think," he concluded with great candor, "that I'd look so pretty in a bottle."

GILBERT MILLSTEIN

On Stage: DIAHANN CARROLL

Diahann Carroll is a popular singer and actress, the essence of whose art is a childlikeness so pervasive as to make her performance seem the enchanting abstraction of a small girl alone in a large room with jalousies, caracoling gravely and delicately before a gilded pier glass in ball gown and tiara, feet bare, arms lifted in slender cartouche, lips parted, back arched, and eyes swimming. In a woman of twenty-five and a recent mother (she is the wife of her manager, Monte Kay, whom she met in 1954 when he was casting director for the musical *House of Flowers,* in which she made her Broadway debut as the tender ingénue, Ottilie), the effect, uncalculated as the green-stick worldliness of very young people, is extraordinary, particularly since both her body and voice are full grown.

Miss Carroll is quite beautiful in the extravagant style of Fayum portraiture. She is a little above middle height and scrupulously rounded; her hair is black; her eyes are the color of Spanish tobacco and set wide above high cheekbones; her skin is a pearled brown; her hands, long and graceful, live a life of their own. Her voice is a light, clear contralto, perfectly projected and purer than that of many more eminent popular vocalists. It is capable of the most surprising growls of seduction, rasps of honest greed, and the expression of all the laments, pleasures, exhortations, serenities, and regrets that make up the vulgate of commercial music.

Adult audiences are drawn to her by the obvious conviction with which she retails these sentiments and by their awareness that she could scarcely have experienced all of them. It is the belief of Ahmet Ertegun, a savant of the record industry, that this quality also makes her attractive to teen-agers, the most important market in the record business. "One thing that's death with kids today," Ertegun observed not long ago, "is a too mature and knowing kind of sound, the blasé, I've-been-through-it-all kind of thing. *Pour les gosses,*" he explained further, "it is *antipathique.*"

This fall, Miss Carroll is in France making the film *Paris Blues*—a Marlon Brando production—which will furnish her with her first starring role, that of a girl who falls in love with an expatriate American jazz musician. She has played minor parts in the motion-picture versions of *Carmen Jones* and *Porgy and Bess* (in both, her physical charms were revealed, but her voice was not, as it was the producers' conceit that other voices be dubbed in for those of Miss Carroll and the principals); she has appeared in numerous television variety shows and has become a successful headliner in such fashionable night clubs as New York's Persian Room; and she has recorded five albums of songs, none of which satisfy her, although all have been reviewed favorably and have sold well. She is a serious-minded girl. "In the last few years," she said recently, "I've been convinced that if a fact sits in the back of your head and you go bravely on as though it weren't there, whatever you're trying to do, you won't, unless you go back and deal with it.

"Well, I never believed in myself as a recording artist and the records show it. I don't like my sound on them. I've always been *visual.*" Her hands strayed briefly about her face and hair until finally the questing fingers took refuge in each other. "I'm stubborn in taking to ideas," she went on. "No one ever told me how to move, what to say, how to say it, or picked my material for me. I do terrible shows sometimes; other times I'm thrilled with something I do. I'm a growing performer. Maybe it's interesting for people to see ideas being experimented with before them. I try to express my curiosity about life—which includes sex—but it's a young curiosity, *wanting* to be in love rather than just hot clawing. I'm not the fiery woman going to run off stage and jump into bed with the nearest man."

Someone once remarked of Miss Carroll, "She reminds me of Thurgood Marshall [chief counsel for the N.A.A.C.P.]: both upper middle class, both fully conscious of civil rights, but both fully assimilated." That she can be so described is largely due to the efforts of her parents, John and Mabel Johnson, Southern-born Negroes who made it their lifework to get their daughter and her sister out of the Harlem ghetto. Her father is a subway conductor who somehow managed to invest in real estate successfully enough to move his family to Yonkers when Carol Diahann was fifteen. "In my part of Harlem," Miss Carroll recalls, "little boys got shot or went to jail, little girls got pregnant, and kids resented anyone who wore a clean blouse every day instead of on every third, and so on." Her parents gave her piano lessons, got her into Manhattan's High School of Music and Art, and did not oppose her when she won a talent contest which put her on television (where she won $3,000) and in show business.

The result is an attitude toward being a Negro that is not usually heard among Negroes and that she now and then exemplifies in terms of theater. "One day," she says, "I'd like very much to be in a sophisticated romantic comedy about, say, two people. Negroes. But not a race play. We'd *laugh* at ourselves, something we haven't learned to do yet."

GILBERT MILLSTEIN

Photograph by MILTON H. GREENE

GIVING NEW LIFE TO OLD MUSIC

The New York Pro Musica

makes an international hit with the

twelfth-century *Play of Daniel*

By RICHARD MURPHY

Ad honorem tui, Christe,
Danielis ludus iste,
In Belvaco est inventus,
Et invenit hunc juventus.

Thus begins *The Play of Daniel:* "In your honor, Christ/ This Daniel Play/ Was written at Beauvais/ The product of our youth"—the product of the twelfth century, that is, written for performance during the Christmas season by the students of the Cathedral of Beauvais. Some eight hundred Christmases had to pass before *Daniel*, rescued from obscurity by a former machinist in the U.S. Merchant Marine, again raised its multiple voice in celebration of the season.

Before a period backdrop, New York's Pro Musica performs Renaissance music at the Festival of Two Worlds in Spoleto, Italy. Instruments being played are, in left group, portative organ, harpsichord, triangle, and bass viol; in right group, recorders, tambourine, finger cymbals (third from right), and drum (in the hands of Director Noah Greenberg, second from right).

That was three years ago in New York City; since then *Daniel* has become a unique international hit. The man who revived the play, Noah Greenberg, last summer took it back to Europe, where it was performed with triumphant success in a succession of notable churches from the small Romanesque church of Sant' Eufemia in Spoleto, Italy, to Westminster Abbey. This winter Chicago, and in the future other cities, will behold its vigorous medieval charms. *The Play of*

Daniel shows signs of becoming a fixture, the most successful venture of a remarkable man and the remarkable group he created—the New York Pro Musica.

Now forty-one, Greenberg is a conductor and musical scholar who for the last eight years has been breathing life into music previously presumed to be thoroughly dead. The first artist to be revived by his ministrations was one Adriano Banchieri, a Bolognese composer of the sixteenth and early seventeenth century who took holy orders at the monastery of San Michele in Bosco, adopted the academic name "Il Dissonante," and produced quantities of religious and secular works in the revolutionary style of his model and friend Claudio Monteverdi. Banchieri is remembered by musicologists as the man who first put the dynamic directions *f* and *p* on a musical score. His other achievements—and they were considerable—would still be lost to the concert-going and record-buying public were it not for the appearance in 1953, on the now-defunct Esoteric label, of a long-playing record titled *Festino, A Renaissance Madrigal Entertainment to be sung "on the Evening of Fat Thursday before Supper."* That recording, by Greenberg and the group then known somewhat formidably as the Primavera Singers of the Pro Musica Antiqua of New York, marked both the return of Banchieri to modest concert-hall recognition and, in a sense, the renaissance of the musical Renaissance.

In what Pro Musica fanciers refer to as the pre-Greenberg era, the performance of ancient music was for the most part in the hands of amateurs who subjected composers like Guillaume Dufay (1400–1474), Josquin des Prés (1445–1521), and Orlando di Lasso (1530–1594) to readings that were reverent, soulful—and almost invariably wrong. To the natural hazards of sketchily annotated music—early composers generally performed and conducted their own music and rarely troubled to score it—was added the tendency on the part of amateur and professional alike to modernize the instrumentation and enhance the sound of ancient music in such a fashion that it was "rendered practical for the abilities of the performers" (a plea originally advanced by the German Carl Friedrich Zelter to explain his mutilation of Bach's *Saint Matthew Passion*). Instrumentation was enriched, the piano was used as a substitute for the harpsichord, the violin did the work of the viol. There were, of course, distinguished groups, notably the Pro Musica Antiqua of Brussels, from which the New York group derived its name (to avoid confusion, Greenberg's group later dropped the "Antiqua"), but their approach to old music tended to be severely scholarly, drained of the dramatic

juices so much of the music clearly demanded. What Greenberg proposed—and brilliantly succeeded in achieving—was a vocal and instrumental group that combined in equal parts first-rate scholarship, dramatic flair, and a high measure of professional competence equal to the virtuoso demands of music before 1700.

The founder and director of the Pro Musica brought impressive if somewhat unorthodox credentials to his job. Raised in New York, in a nonmusical family, he studied piano as a youngster, learned composition privately, and soon developed a passion for early music. He never attended college. From 1942 to 1949 he sailed with the Merchant Marine as a master machinist, taking advantage of trips to Italy and France to pick up rare scores and recordings at various ports of call. When he left the sea and returned to New York, Greenberg had a first-rate knowledge of early music and some shrewdly thought-out ideas about how it should be performed. What he lacked was money, contacts, and a public platform on which to exercise his talents. For a time he worked for the International Ladies Garment Workers Union (he had become an active trade unionist during his days at sea), organizing some of the members into amateur choruses, one of which made a specialty of early music.

In 1952 Esoteric Records heard about his efforts. Like many another small company in the early days of the LP boom, Esoteric was casting about for repertory that had not been thoroughly raked over by the giants of the industry. Renaissance music was an obvious answer, and Greenberg, already highly regarded by its devotees, was an obvious man to conduct it. When he agreed to cut an album, Greenberg insisted that he be allowed to select professional musicians for his ensemble—he was already far too familiar with the mutilations practiced by amateurs—and that Esoteric provide enough money to train the ensemble in proper Renaissance style. He believed then, as he believes now, that early music, with its odd intervals and generally taxing vocal lines, demands at least as much of its performers as the most prickly effusions of the Schönberg school.

For the New York Pro Musica's production of The Play of Daniel, *W. H. Auden (left) wrote a verse narration; Greenberg (right) scored the work for voices and instruments.*

This thirteenth-century manuscript, in the Egerton Collection of the British Museum, was the source from which the music of The Play of Daniel, a single melodic line, was transcribed into modern notation.

Greenberg recruited six vocalists, the most unique of whom was the splendid countertenor Russell Oberlin, who had been singing with Robert Shaw's Collegiate Chorale and who, by his own testimony, had not been aware until he met Greenberg that "there *was* such music." In addition to Oberlin there were two sopranos, a contralto, a tenor, and a bass. To these Greenberg added Blanche Winogron, a virtuoso player of the virginals (a sixteenth-century keyboard instrument related to the spinet and harpsichord, whose name, some authorities have suggested, derived from its popularity with young ladies), and set her to playing interludes by Joanambrosio Dalza, Girolamo Frescobaldi, and Giovanni Gabrieli. The happy result of this first collaboration was Banchieri's entertainment for a Fat Thursday's eve.

Esoteric shortly thereafter went out of business, presumably for reasons other than its addiction to Renaissance music, but Greenberg's Pro Musica continued to thrive as both a recording and a concert-hall group. The basic concert ensemble now comprises the six-singer vocal group (though most of the original singers, including Oberlin, have since left and a baritone takes the place of the contralto) plus four instrumentalists. Since each of the instrumentalists is master of more than a single instrument, and since the vocalists also all perform on medieval percussion instruments—triangles, drums, hand bells, and finger cymbals—the ensemble is capable of a considerably wider range of effects than might be expected of so small a group. When larger forces are required, Greenberg relies on outside recruits, such as the boy choristers of Manhattan's Church of the Transfiguration.

The ensemble, all of whose members are loyal constituents of Local 802 of the American Federation of Musicians, performs in immaculate evening dress in accordance with a dictum early laid down by Greenberg: "If we appeared in medieval dress, we'd pack them in in Toledo, but it would distract attention from the music." The ensemble gives a dozen or so concerts in Manhattan annually and upwards of fifty concerts on the road. It is Greenberg's particular pride that most of the concerts are sold out well in advance and that the group is as well received in Peoria or Waco as it is in New York. The Pro Musica draws a great many young people, and Greenberg has discovered, not surprisingly, that lovers of modern music are among the most ardent admirers of the old.

The Pro Musica's field of interest spans roughly five centuries—1200 to 1700—from Gregorian chant to Henry Purcell. Within that rewarding range the group has mastered an

TEXT CONTINUED ON PAGE 94

PHOTOGRAPHS CLAUDE MICHAELIDES

Last summer, the New York Pro Musica toured Europe with its production of The Play of Daniel, *presenting it at many music festivals and in such churches as the severely Roman-esque Sant' Eufemia, at Spoleto (opposite page), and the Gothic Abbey of Royaumont in the diocese of Beauvais (photographs above and at right), where* The Play of Daniel *was originally produced for Christmas about the year 1150.*

TEXT CONTINUED FROM PAGE 91

impressive repertory—English madrigals and songs, French Renaissance music and compositions of the Italian Baroque, music of medieval Spain and Germany. Some of the composers bear familiar names: William Byrd, Thomas Tallis, Cristóbal de Morales, Heinrich Schütz, and Giovanni Pierluigi, called "da Palestrina." Others are anonymous or are little more than footnotes to musical history: Tobias Hume, the seventeenth-century composer of *Captaine Hume's Poeticall Musicke,* who posed as a colonel in the army and died in poverty after offering his services to the House of Lords against the Irish rebels; Alonso Mudarra, a lute-song composer of the sixteenth century, who published somber variations on Spanish popular tunes and ballads, including one on the siege of Antequera; Martin de Rivaflecha, *maestro da capilla* at the Cathedral of Palencia, who died in 1528 and is remembered for his mystical mingling of plain chant and polyphony in the antiphon *Salve Regina.*

To set the echoes of such music ringing vividly in the contemporary ear requires not only scholarship but a journey of the imagination. The problem with pre-Bach music in its surviving forms is often not that it is too complex but that it is too simple: little is indicated beyond the basic melodic line; tempo, rhythm, and instrumentation are left to the ingenuity of the performers. Greenberg's reconstruction of such music is based on a knowledge of its period, the advice of musicologists, and intuitive good taste. What emerges is not, of course, the "correct" performance, but it should be one that is historically possible and even probable. It should also, Greenberg feels, be a genuine "performance," fresh and theatrically arresting, rather than a piece of auricular scholarship. Much of the music with which the Pro Musica deals, even the church music, was popular entertainment, and it can suffer from too much caution as well as too little care.

The sound of the past lives in its instruments. To re-create this sound, the Pro Musica has built a collection that comprises most of the major instruments of the Renaissance. Sometimes the group uses surviving originals, such as the straight trumpet on which are engraved the name Siena and the date 1406; more often, it employs reproductions, made to Greenberg's order by European craftsmen. They include the cromorne, a hook-shaped wood-wind instrument of the sixteenth and seventeenth centuries that lent its name to the cromorna reed stop on the organ; the zinke, a wood-wind instrument with a cup mouthpiece, which had a great vogue in the sixteenth and seventeenth centuries and then disappeared into sudden obscurity; the portative organ, a fourteenth-century instrument small enough to hold in the lap, which was copied for Greenberg after an instrument in a Van Eyck painting. The Pro Musica is also equipped with viols, recorders, harpsichords, tuned hand bells, the ten-stringed psaltery, and the pear-shaped rebec.

The Pro Musica's most impressive feat of revival is, of course, *The Play of Daniel.* Greenberg's reconstruction of the play is based on a thirteenth-century manuscript of whose existence in the British Museum he became aware in 1954 after reading the music of *Daniel* in Edouard de Coussemaker's *Drames liturgiques du moyen-âge.* In its manuscript form, *Daniel's* music consists of a single melodic line; Father Rembert Weakland, O.S.B., was called upon to transcribe it into modern notation. Greenberg himself did the scoring and editing for voices and instruments. In this task he was aided in part by the internal evidence of the Latin verse, as when the procession of the entering Queen sings: ". . . with sonorous tones of strings and voices let music now be made." His choice of specific instruments was dictated by his knowledge of the symbolism of medieval instrumentation: the psaltery and minstrel's harp, for instance, were considered sacred and were therefore used in the presence of Daniel; the rebec and cymbal, connoting evil, were appropriate to the envious counselors. As first performed in the Romanesque Hall of The Cloisters (the uptown, medieval branch of New York's Metropolitan Museum), *Daniel* employed, in addition to the above instruments, such exotica as the minstrel's harp, the portative organ and an assortment of recorders; the twelve soloists were supported by eight boy choristers.

Lincoln Kirstein supervised the entire production—the staging and direction as well as the costumes, which were derived mostly from illuminated manuscripts and partly from the figures on the west front of the Cathedral of Chartres. To guide the audience through the complexities of the medieval Latin and French dialogue, W. H. Auden supplied an English verse narration, for delivery by an actor costumed as a monk, which not only outlines the action but evokes for a contemporary audience the emotional context in which the prophet Daniel lived.

The play (based on episodes from the Book of Daniel in the Vulgate) unfolds with linear simplicity: the prophet Daniel predicts the overthrow of Belshazzar, becomes counselor to the conquering Darius, is betrayed and cast into the lions' den from which he is liberated, exalted in his conviction that there is a time when ". . . the holy one comes/ The most holy of the holy." The charm of the work lies in its simple, melodious music, suggestive of everything from folk song to Gregorian chant, and in the splendid pageantry with which the Pro Musica invests its childlike visions. There are Oriental suggestions, echoes of the Crusades in the stately, cymbal-punctuated opening procession honoring Belshazzar's "comely" Queen. There are scenes of unfettered rejoicing to the fluttering recorders, moments of quiet reverence summoned by the tenderly piping boy sopranos, sudden pangs of anguish in the moments of Daniel's farewell. The moods are as transient as sunlight—and as freshly appealing as the season in which they were born.

As the music editor of Time, *Richard Murphy comments on a host of performers and performances. His interests are also literary, manifested by book reviews and a novel in progress.*

"*So Daniel is down in the deep pit,
Alone among lions. But the Lord of Heaven
Sends an angel with a sword to keep
Those beasts at bay that they bite him not.
And a second angel He sends in the night
To Habakkuk, a holy prophet,
Saying: 'Arise! The road is long.
I am bid to bring you to Babylon town
And the dark den where Daniel lies.'
'That is full far,' says that faithful man,
'And I know not the way; nevertheless
I will go to greet him.' God's angel
Takes him by the hair; in a trice they come
To the perilous pit; he appears to Daniel,
Refreshes with food his fainting spirit.*"

*. . . Thus intones the monk-narrator in W.
H. Auden's verse for* The Play of Daniel
*just after the prophet has been cast into the
lions' den by the jealous satraps of King
Darius. At right is the scene as staged in the
Pro Musica's first production at The Cloisters in New York. It is followed by the
song of Daniel when he observes the angel
of the Lord who comes to hold the beasts at
bay. A memorable illustration of this epi-
sode is that from the* Apocalypse of St. Sever
*(below), a celebrated 11th-century French
manuscript. Robert Fletcher, who created
the sumptuous costumes for* Daniel, *based
his designs on such medieval illuminations.*

SERVICE PHOTOGRAPHIQUE, BIBLIOTHEQUE NATIONALE

95

A 1940 news picture of Dr. Rosenbach with a Second Folio

THE CONQUESTS OF
Dr. Rosenbach

Business titans competed for the honor of buying First Folios from a genial Napoleon of book collecting whose finds were as phenomenal as the prices he got for them

By EDWIN WOLF 2ND *with* JOHN F. FLEMING

Although the world of the antiquarian bookseller is not generally linked in the public mind with moments of high drama and suspense, it was so in the early decades of this century when Dr. A. S. W. Rosenbach of Philadelphia and New York dominated it. Brilliant scholar, discoverer, and psychologist of taste, and a showman of lively originality besides, he lent to it an excitement it had not had before—and has not had since. Living in the greatest age of private book collecting, he, perhaps more than anyone else, stimulated American millionaires to acquire treasures that have since passed over in large part into institutional, educational hands for the benefit of many. The story of his engaging life is told in a new book, *Rosenbach: A Biography,* by Edwin Wolf 2nd with John F. Fleming, to be published this month by The World Publishing Company. The authors were associates of the late Dr. Rosenbach for more than twenty years, Mr. Wolf as manager of the parent store in Philadelphia, Mr. Fleming as assistant to the Doctor in New York. From their book the excerpts on the following pages are drawn, with short editorial passages introducing individual episodes.

Abraham Simon Wolf Rosenbach had plump pink cheeks, a twinkle in his eye, walked—as a friend once said—as a penguin would walk if a penguin could walk like Rosy, puffed everlastingly on a pipe or cigar, drank a bottle of whisky a day, and was the greatest antiquarian bookseller the world has seen. Without much pressing he would admit as much.

"The Doctor," as he was familiarly known to collector-friends and employees, for decades bought most of the important rare books and manuscripts sold at auction in England and America. It was not just that he paid more money for books than anyone had before, but that the buying and selling were the manifestations of a faith in the greatness of great books that he persuaded other men to share. His faith was contagious beyond the small circle of men who could buy a book collection or a railroad with equal aplomb. To Dr. Rosenbach, more than to any other person, the rare-book libraries of the United States owe, if not always their books, the philosophical concept of the importance of rare books, which has been the basis of their successful growth.

The world knew him as the Napoleon of the auction room, the man who set record prices year after year. He was the unbeatable bidder who paid £8,600 for a First Folio of Shakespeare in 1922 and £14,500 for another copy in 1933, who bought a Gutenberg Bible for $106,000 and a Bay Psalm Book for $151,000, who went up to $51,000 for a document signed by the elusive signer of the Declaration of Independence, Button Gwinnett, and who purchased for £15,400 the original manuscript of *Alice in Wonderland*.

From a modest little gift shop established in Philadelphia at the turn of the century by his brother Philip, with funds generously provided by a lady friend (who was, in turn, the dear friend of a Philadelphia sugar baron), the great firm of The Rosenbach Company grew. In 1903, "Abie," who had just received a doctorate in Elizabethan literature from the University of Pennsylvania, formally entered the business. He opened a rare-book department, and the fortunes of the firm took a sharp upswing. By 1915, after years of careful buying with little capital, the Doctor had built up a sizable clientele, with whom he was on the most friendly terms, and a backlog of books which was to come in very handy in the boom years just beginning.

Hindsight is one of the cheapest of commodities. Dr. Rosenbach had his share of it, but his foresight was so keen that he did not have to solace himself with what might have been. When the Elizabethans came into their own, when Americana was valued as he always hoped it would be, the Doctor crested with the waves. These were the golden, early summer days of eighteenth- and nineteenth-century authors. A bird in the hand was worth a bag of prophecies.

The bird, to give an instance early in Dr. Rosenbach's career, was the "Sentimental Library" of Harry B. Smith. The sentimentalist, who had made his reputation in the theatrical world, had for twenty years been gathering a collection of "books which are interesting on account of their associations and books which have been made unique by the addition of letters or manuscripts." It was, indeed, a great aggregation of conversation pieces—the *Pickwick* which Dickens had presented to his wife's sister, Mary Hogarth, whose death caused the publication of Part XV to be postponed because of the author's emotional collapse; the copy of *Essays of Elia* which Lamb presented to Fanny Kelly, to whom he had proposed marriage, and as a sympathetic pendant (for the gentle Elia never married), the manuscript of "Dream Children"; the very copy of *Queen Mab* which Shelley gave to Mary Godwin with a poignant note inside the back cover: "You see, Mary, I have not forgotten you"; the manuscript of Keats's sonnet "On First Looking into Chapman's Homer"—books, manuscripts, letters, and relics, each with the aura of the author, physical fragments of his immortality.

The Doctor's flattering letters to Smith had smoothed his way, and his audacity in seeking to buy a major collection when other dealers were moaning about the effects of World War I opened the door. The crux of the situation was cash. No dealer had enough ready money to swing a deal of that size, certainly not the Rosenbachs. The Doctor, however, realized that all one needed in order to get money was a combination of bravado and friends.

He had both. When he approached his friend William M. Elkins with the suggestion that his banking house lend The Rosenbach Company the $79,000 needed to buy the Smith library, he spoke to the heart of a collector prejudiced in his favor. The agreement was reached. Elkins, Morris and Company would put up the purchase price as a loan; interest would be paid on what was outstanding, and the loan would be reduced monthly as sales were made. Compared to later ventures conducted in the same manner —and these were the basis of Dr. Rosenbach's phenomenal success—the Smith library did not pay off over a short term. Nonetheless, the purchase of the "Sentimental Library" taught the Doctor how libraries could be bought with friendly financing. Even more important, the announcement of the purchase, tinkling through the sound of the siege guns at Verdun, raised A. S. W. Rosenbach sensationally and immediately above the ruck of antiquarian book dealers. He had made his first major coup.

In February, 1918, the Rosenbach brothers leased the second, third, and fourth floors of the neighboring linen shop to turn into more showrooms for the steadily growing stock of furniture, paintings, and *objets d'art*. While the galleries were being hung with the paintings of their star attraction, Joseph Pennell, Dr. Rosenbach was trying to make a difficult decision: how large a bid to send to secure the only surviving letter written by Amerigo Vespucci, the man who gave his name to two continents. It was to be sold as part of the Alfred Morrison collection, the greatest collection of autographs ever auctioned in London. The Doctor had sent a few small bids at one of the sessions (of the sale), but as Dr. Rosenbach later recalled, the critical months at the beginning of 1918 found the buying public preoccupied with only one subject—the war. Although Dr. R. was fully aware that the book market was sadly depressed, he could not hope that a unique letter which had survived the wars of more than four centuries would fall to him at an upset price. It was, no doubt of it, one of the greatest American manuscripts ever put up for auction. With trepidation he sent off a bid of £1,100.

Ten thousand dollars would not have been an exorbitant price for it; to his utter delight Dr. Rosenbach got the cabled news that it was his for £390. He always considered the purchase of the Vespucci letter one of the greatest bargains of his career.

The price was only the first of two miracles. When the letter arrived, the Doctor went over it carefully. It was a serious formal epistle which young Amerigo wrote in Latin to his father in 1476. In it he commented on a commonplace book—the kind of book in which men wrote down phrases, sentences, or passages they wanted to remember—that had belonged to his uncle, Giorgio

97

Antonio Vespucci. For a moment Dr. Rosenbach sat bemused, and then something clicked in his memory. He jumped from his chair, rushed to a bookcase, skimmed quickly along a shelf, and pulled out an old manuscript in a fifteenth-century binding. It was a commonplace book and on the first page was the name of Giorgio Antonio Vespucci. The arm of coincidence, like the time machine of science fiction, operates through the centuries. Separated for almost half a millennium, the book and the letter were miraculously together in the hands of a bookseller in a land still unknown when they were written.

With the end of the war, Dr. Rosenbach stood on the threshold of his greatest days. When the Rhode Island collector of Shakespeareana Marsden J. Perry decided bitterly to sell his collection rather than stand by while two new collectors, Henry C. Folger and Henry E. Huntington, built better ones, Dr. Rosenbach was ready. There was the nagging problem of financing. But with adroit management of his friends the Wideners, and another loan from William Elkins, the Perry collection, valued at $600,000, went to Dr. Rosenbach for a bid of $250,000.

Dr. Rosenbach was determined to make the Perry collection a landmark in the history of bookselling. It was, in a way, to be his proof of the potentiality of the scholar-dealer. A seller who knew that Lodge's *Rosalynde* was the basic source of *As You Like It* could be expected to sell it for more than another to whom it was only a rare piece of merchandise. A scholar who could tell the story of Mistress Arden and her paramour Mosbie, who hired Black Will and Shakbag to kill Arden of Feversham, could persuade a customer that the first edition of the play based on that crime—a play attributed to Shakespeare—was a book he could not afford to pass up. When A. S. W. Rosenbach went to see a customer, he was more than a salesman peddling his wares, he was a man saturated with the books he wanted to sell.

Henry C. Folger was chosen to get the greatest prize of the Perry collection. "Chosen" is used advisedly, for certainly Huntington (another big customer) would have been interested in it; and possibly others, too, might have risen to the occasion—and the book. The stubby quarto volume with Edward Gwynne's name stamped on its old calf cover contained nine plays by or attributed to Shakespeare. The book was the only complete copy known of the first tentative attempt at the publication of a collected edition of Shakespeare's plays. As the Doctor informed Folger categorically, when congratulating him upon his purchase, it was THE FINEST SHAKESPEAREAN VOLUME IN EXISTENCE. Apart from the fact that Mr. Folger could afford to pay a handsome price, Rosenbach reasoned that it belonged in the greatest Shakespearean collection in formation.

Although Dr. Rosenbach told Folger it was a volume upon which "no price can be placed," he did manage to figure out that he could sell it in a lot for $128,500. Yet the rest of the "lot" was not baser alloy by any means. Next to a less spectacular volume than the Gwynne quarto, they would have been dazzling in their own light: the only copy in America (and one of three known) of the earliest form of *Henry VI, Part 2* as it was printed in 1594; the only known fragment of the third edition of *Venus and Adonis*, 1595, and one of two copies known of the 1636 edition; one of two copies known of the *Pericles* of 1611; Admiral Penn's copy of *Richard III*, 1605; Charles Lamb's copy of Shakespeare's *Poems*; and a number of other items.

When A. S. W. Rosenbach went in to see Mr. Huntington in midsummer of 1919, Huntington got a rich—if second—selection of Perry books. The lot included the third edition of Lodge's *Rosalynde*, 1596 (a unique, imperfect copy of the first edition of 1590 appeared in the Britwell collection, and except for the two English institutional copies of the second edition, no others are known to this day); the first *Arden of Feversham*, 1592 (the last copy to appear for sale and still the only one in America); the Shakespeare source play *The Second Part of the troublesome Raigne of King John*, 1591; and *The Rape of Lucrece*, 1632.

Then the Doctor went to see Charles W. Clark in Los Angeles, and he took a few books. En route he stopped in San Francisco, where Templeton Crocker bought $17,885 worth, including a Second Folio for $5,750 and a Third for $11,750—certainly the highest prices either of those books ever had been sold for. By the time Dr. Rosenbach stepped off the train in Philadelphia, at the end of August, he had sold nearly $350,000 worth of Perry books. He had accomplished this in three months.

At this point, the Doctor was ready publicly to announce its purchase. "For a price said to exceed $500,000," newspapers throughout the world reported, the Philadelphia bookseller had bought the greatest Shakespeare collection in private hands. The star items were described, and much was made of the Gwynne volume, sold to Folger for $100,000, said to be the highest-priced book in the world.

The Doctor, however, had made a serious mistake in permitting the Folger information to leak to the newspapers, for within a few days after the story broke, the gentle collector, genuinely annoyed, called on Rosenbach and demanded that thereafter he refrain from giving any publicity whatsoever to his purchases. Folger went on to explain, with characteristic amiability, why he was chary of publicity.

He had been playing golf with the elder John D. Rockefeller in Florida. As they were walking off a green, the old man turned and remarked softly, "Henry, I see from the papers that you just paid $100,000 for a book!" Folger felt a sinking feeling in the pit of his stomach, but in the best tradition of book collectors through the ages, he recovered and said quickly, "Now, John. You know better than that. If you buy something for $10,000, it becomes $100,000 in print." There was a moment's pause; perhaps the wise old man was unwilling to pursue so delicate a subject as money. Then he said, "Well, I'm glad to hear you say that, Henry. We—that is, my son and I and the board of directors—were disturbed. We wouldn't want to think that the president of one of our major companies [Folger was then head of Standard Oil of New York] would be the kind of man foolish enough to pay $100,000 for a book!"

Not the least of the Doctor's talents was his ability to do business on a personal level, to create the impression that he was doing a client a favor by selling him a book. He always looked upon himself not as a man in trade but as a gentleman, and his wealthy customers took him at his own evaluation. This state of affairs, however, sometimes led the Doctor into a difficult pass; in a few cases, it brought him to the brink of catastrophe.

One day, in the late spring of 1922, he was dining with the famous collector William A. White, in Brooklyn. The talk that evening was, of course, about books. White and the Doctor stood in the library pulling down one thin volume after another from the shelves, swapping stories, noting points, and recalling prices.

When Mr. White handed the Doctor his unique copy of the third edition of *Richard II*, 1598, he asked, "What do you think this little book is worth?" "Fifty thousand dollars," Dr. Rosenbach answered impetuously. "Would you give that for it?" White countered. "I think I would," the dealer said, a bit less impetuously. "Well, I'm glad to know your opinion," said White. "In 1890 I paid $348 for it." With that the subject was dropped, but the book talk went on. As the Doctor was about to take his leave, quite late, his host looked at him innocently and asked, "Aren't you going to take that book with you? I've never sold a Shakespeare quarto in my life, but I'm sorely tempted. I'm itching to tell my skeptical family that I wasn't such a fool when I invested money in what they considered playthings." To A. S. W. Rosenbach that was a challenge; he took the book.

Arnold Toynbee has stated that civilizations progress by their responses to challenges. So did the Doctor. For $50,000 less 10 per cent, a fantastic sum, he had a third edition, not a first, of a Shakespeare quarto of which the earlier two editions were, by Rosenbach standards, common—in 1922 three copies of the first were known and eight of the second. In a letter to Henry Folger, marked "Very Confidential," he set forth his case. "With the exception of the *Titus Andronicus*, 1594, it is the *only unique* Shakespeare quarto published in the 16th century," he told the collector. "I am only permitted to offer it to you and Mr. Huntington, and I am making you the first offer. One of the reasons that has influenced me to do this is that you are the only private collector that already possesses a unique Shakespeare quarto, the *Titus Andronicus*. Mr. Huntington has not had the good fortune to possess any." Huntington was in town, he warned his rival, so it would be wise if Folger could see Rosenbach at once. Two days later, Folger acquired his second unique quarto for $55,000; the Doctor, taking his commission both ways, made $10,000; and White made one of the largest book profits on record.

As the market for rare books boomed, Doctor Rosenbach found it increasingly difficult to supply his star customers. He was dismayed by Huntington's large purchases in the art field, and to stem the flow of money into the hands of his archrival, the great art dealer Sir Joseph Duveen, he was driven to new expedients. He began cultivating people in strategic places, such as Huntington's secretary, Hapgood, and he greatly increased the volume of his activity in London, where most of his greatest purchases were made. He spread his net so wide that, now and then, the most extraordinary things tumbled into it.

In 1924, after gathering all the private plums ready to fall at auction and privately negotiated transactions, Dr. Rosenbach descended on the London bookstores. Until this time he had not felt secure enough to buy extensively and outright from other dealers. It had been his practice to take most books from English dealers on consignment, sometimes paying for them years after the items had been sold and, as dilatorily, returning those for which no buyer had been found. But now the Doctor felt he had to build up his stock. He was amazed that London dealers were so naïve about prices. Their shelves were loaded with bargains—incunables that would sweeten future lists for Huntington, Elizabethan books that were selling for bargain prices, an American item here and there that he could salt away, letters of the English literary greats for a growing host of American autograph

collectors, and occasionally an unusual volume which was spirited away into his own collection. He went from store to store, buying with an open hand. Yet in spite of his willingness to pay good prices, none of the English dealers was very fond of the Doctor. He never had any close friends among them, as Alfred Quaritch had been in his youth, and his relationships with them, although outwardly cordial, were merely polite. He bought heavily, paid slowly, boasted unceasingly, and stole the best books in England right from under their noses.

It was from the strait-laced firm of Maggs Brothers that Dr. Rosenbach secured his prize purchase. For £400 he bought from them the collection of Napoleon relics carefully treasured by the Abbé Vignali. Vignali was one of two Corsican priests sent by the former Emperor's uncle, Cardinal Fesch, to conduct religious services for him at St. Helena. The second priest stayed but a short time; Vignali remained with Napoleon until he died. Apart from specific items willed to different individuals, a number of objects were, according to mutual agreement by Napoleon's companions-in-exile, divided among them. A share went to Vignali, and it was his share—with curious additions—that the Doctor purchased and brought home with much fanfare. Napoleon's silver knife, fork, and spoon with the imperial arms, his silver cup, a fine holland shirt, which the Emperor was said to have worn during the last days of his illness, a handkerchief marked with his cipher, the famous white breeches—these and a few other odds and ends were the usual things that collectors of relics, among whom Dr. Rosenbach was never numbered, swooned over.

But what gave spice to the collection—and to the Doctor's conversation for a quarter of a century afterward—was an unpleasant-looking piece of desiccated tissue, politely described as "a mummified tendon taken from Napoleon's body during the postmortem." A memoir by St. Denis, published in the *Revue des Deux Mondes*, confirmed its authenticity. St. Denis expressly stated that he and Vignali took away small pieces of Napoleon's corpse during the autopsy. No collector's item was ever shown with more spicy delight than this sad remnant of the glory of a Napoleon who had written passionately that he would cover his Josephine "with a million kisses burning as though beneath the equator." Few so intimate portions of a man's anatomy have ever been displayed to so many. Alas, poor Bonaparte! It is surprising that with his flair for the dramatic the Doctor never hit upon the idea of returning the "tendon" to the French to be interred officially with the rest of Napoleon's remains in Les Invalides.

To the eminent Boston physician Dr. Harvey Cushing, who returned a book because he would not pay four times what it had fetched when Rosenbach bought it in London, the Doctor wrote testily: "I do not consider 400% a large profit, or 10,000% large. We place a price on the volume based on what we consider its worth, regardless of its cost. Customers evidently agree with us, as we have a numerous clientele, as you know, the world over." What he really had, however, was a number of big clients; he could never bring himself to develop a large number of small ones. He also discriminated between prospective customers, refusing to make a large sale on at least one occasion because he felt the man did not "deserve" the book. But his dependence on a few men like Huntington, White, and Folger meant that he was in an extremely vulnerable position if relations with them went slightly awry. In 1924 a slip occurred in the New York office that might have changed the story of the life of A. S. W. Rosenbach if he had not arranged his affairs to deal with the contingency.

While the Doctor was in Philadelphia, two lots of incunables, destined for the Huntington Library and priced at $98,000 and $100,000, were being checked and listed in New York. With the lists were the bills from the various dealers from whom Rosenbach had bought the items included, lists which were to be sent back to the bookkeeping department in Philadelphia. An assistant packed up the shipment; and in a moment of incredible aberration, he enclosed the bills from the dealers in the letter destined for the Huntington Library.

To Mr. Huntington's librarian, Leslie E. Bliss, who was continually scrutinizing lists, prices, and invoices to catch the Doctor in a minor error, those bills would have been the chance of a lifetime. Dr. Rosenbach never denied that he made a handsome profit, but it was another matter for a valued customer to have chapter and verse on how handsome that profit was. When the Doctor returned to New York the next day, the awful blunder was reported to him. For half an hour he raged and swore like the devil incarnate. By the end of the next half hour he had made arrangements for an unexpected trip to San Marino. If he was to retain Huntington as a client—in fact, if he was to remain the king of the rare-book world—he had to get to California before that letter did. For the first time in his life he conquered his innate physical cowardice and risked traveling in a plane.

No word came back from the Coast except that he had arrived. No hint was given whether the letter or he had arrived first. Philip and the staff tried to imagine what had happened. Ten days later, the Doctor, travel-worn but relaxed, walked into his Madison Avenue store. To the obvious question, he responded with his most charming grin and the laconic statement, "I got there just in time. It cost me over a thousand dollars." Certainly Philip was told what had occurred and how he retrieved the letter, but no one else ever knew. Among expense vouchers for the year appeared an otherwise unexplained payment of $1,000 to friend Hapgood, Huntington's obliging secretary.

Dr. Rosenbach's international reputation and a large part of his fame at home were based on his performance at the London auction house of Sotheby's, where over many years he bought virtually all the best offerings and paid spectacular sums for them. It became the custom of London newspapers to report that "unless otherwise noted," sales of books at Sotheby's went to Dr. Rosenbach. In 1925, for example, when the Doctor declined to bid on a famous Chaucer manuscript, the London newspapers considered it as much news as if he had. "Can it be," queried the Evening Standard, *"that Dr. Rosenbach having spent £160,000 in four weeks is beginning to get what I believe his countrymen call 'cold feet'?" The Doctor, who was on the point of making one of the biggest coups of his career, and feeling anything but bearish, was wrestling with a familiar problem: an unparalleled opportunity to buy and a shortage of cash.*

Dr. Rosenbach had, of course, known of the Holford collection by reputation. It had been formed about the middle of the nineteenth century by Robert Stayner Holford, who was better known as a great collector of paintings and engravings. His son, Lieutenant-Colonel Sir George Holford, did not inherit his father's love of books. Fortunately for Dr. Rosenbach, Sir George's taste ran to orchids. Fortunately also for the Doctor, it was an ex-

pensive hobby, and what with the tax situation and the increasing demands of the orchids for care and comfort, Sir George was inclined to consider selling some of the books, which were of no real interest to him.

In April, 1925, Dr. Rosenbach was invited to Dorchester House to see the books. Since the idea of selling his books had already occurred to the orchid-grower, the Doctor's task was not to convince him that he should sell, but that he should sell the pick of them to him. If the Doctor was a persuasive talker at ordinary times, the sight of the Holford collection lent him the seductive tongue of Mephistopheles. He saw on the shelves volumes whose tremendous importance and magnificent condition topped even his hitherto topless towers of superlatives. The matter quickly got to the point: which books and what price. With his uncanny ability to skim through a whole library and pick the best, Dr. Rosenbach selected just over a hundred titles, made a brief list of them, and told Sir George that he would have to figure out what he could afford to pay.

Back in his room at the Carlton, the Doctor sat down and began to jot down figures alongside the titles. His mathematical problem was to guess what he could sell the books for. There was one other problem: Where was he going to get the money to pay for them? Of course he never mentioned this second imponderable to Sir George, who thought that the Rosenbachs had a first lien on the United States Treasury. The Doctor estimated that the selling prices totaled more than a million dollars, and he felt that at half that figure he could safely buy the lot. For £110,000 he got an option on his choice, promising Sir George settlement when he took delivery within three months.

The books were to be packed immediately and sent to a warehouse. Since neither Holford nor the Doctor wanted anyone to know what was occurring, the books, covered with brown paper, were smuggled out of the house in a butcher's cart. Although Dr. Rosenbach over and over again bought and sold "the greatest books in the world," neither he nor anyone else bought greater books than the Holford hundred, which were trundled along the streets of London disguised as legs of mutton.

The hastily scrawled, almost impressionistic list that Dr. Rosenbach made of them reads like an epic of bibliophilism. The Shakespeare items were a saga in themselves. The Four Folios were there, all in original bindings, but the First was the gem—clean, crisp, and perfect in every respect. It was, indeed, a miracle of preservation, and three hundred and two years after it first appeared, Dr. Rosenbach excitedly scribbled the figure of $100,000 next to its brief title on the list. On that list only one title had no price next to it, and that because the Doctor, hardened as he was to the high finance of pricing, could not steel himself to committing to paper a figure as high as the one which was flashing through his mind. The single most valuable book in the Holford lot was the second edition of *Venus and Adonis*, 1594. If a fourth edition of *Venus and Adonis* had been worth the equivalent of $60,000 in the dark ages of 1919, what was a second edition worth in the renaissance of 1925? The Doctor was not ready to answer that question, even to himself. There were yet other Shakespeare treasures on the shelves of Dorchester House, and Dr. Rosenbach took them all. They included the *Rape of Lucrece* and six plays in their first printing, among them *Troilus and Cressida*, 1609—an uncut copy, the only Shakespeare quarto issued during his lifetime to survive in that condition. Another eeven early quartos made up the lot, not first editions, but in some cases the first available edition, like the *Romeo and Juliet* of 1599. Never again would such Shakespeares come into the hands of a dealer.

The Holford purchase, which included many treasures besides the Shakespeares, was so fantastic that the Doctor realized he had better say nothing about it for the moment. Besides, he had no clear idea of how he was going to raise the money to pay for it, although his fertile brain was beginning to cast up alternative ways and means. On May 19, 1925, Dr. A. S. W. Rosenbach, not so cool but very calculating, landed in New York.

He promptly entrained for the West, warning Mr. Huntington in California that he had better send a truck to meet him because he was bringing a trunk full of books. By the time he got there his pent-up excitement was at the boiling point. He got right down to business. From the trunk came a selection of his recent miscellaneous purchases, for which Henry Huntington gave the Doctor a check for $61,250.

Then Dr. Rosenbach really began to talk. He told Mr. Huntington what a wonderful opportunity he had in the Holford books, if Mr. Huntington would help. He described them, but not all of them, as though they lay on the table before them. He sang their praises, describing condition, rarity, and supreme importance. All he needed was the money. Obligingly, Mr. Huntington agreed to finance the transaction.

For $350,000—the largest single sale Dr. Rosenbach had up to that time made—thirty Holford books (including the fabulous *Venus and Adonis*), plus a bonus of eighty-three assorted incunables from other sources, went *de jure* into the Huntington collection, although *de facto* they were still in London not yet settled for.

The sale, however, was only part of Dr. Rosenbach's mission. He had sold Huntington less than a third of the Holford books, sight unseen, and he still needed almost $185,000 to be able to take delivery of the rest. So he persuaded the Californian to purchase a draft for £110,000—which came to $534,875—and cable it to London on his behalf. Then he deducted $350,000 from that sum, paid $61,250 by re-endorsing Huntington's check for that amount back to him, and gave him a 5 per cent, six-month note of The Rosenbach Company for $123,625. The statement of this transaction, sent to New York after the Doctor left Pasadena, showed that he had not in fact settled the account in full; the Rosenbachs still owed Mr. Huntington $3.50 for the cable.

On one point the Doctor and Huntington were agreed: they both wanted to build up the Huntington collection as quickly as possible—Huntington because he was ailing and felt he might not have much time left to do it, and the Doctor because he felt he might run out of books. Folger, in receipt of a price list from Rosenbach, remarked, "Frankly, the prices stagger me." They staggered Huntington, too, but he paid them willingly.

Ordinarily his fellow bibliophiles would have tried to work up a bookman's feast on the occasion of a rare visit to the East from the great Henry E. Huntington, but in the autumn of 1925 his arrival was heralded in the most lugubrious tones. Mr. Huntington, who had been unwell for quite a while, had entered the Lankenau Hospital to be operated on by the Philadelphia surgeon Dr. John B. Deaver. Dr. Rosenbach was in constant attendance, ready to carry out Huntington's every wish. Just before the critical day, he was informed that Mr. Huntington would like to see him.

The same message had been delivered to Sir Joseph Duveen, who had rushed to Philadelphia as soon as the news of his patron's illness reached him. With a concern which equaled that of Dr. Rosenbach, Duveen appeared in the hospital corridor to join the bookseller. They had nothing to talk about except the state of Mr. Huntington's health, and that subject exhausted, they fretted restlessly together in silence. There was no love lost between these two giants. They had sense enough not to interfere with each other, but no helping hand was ever extended by Sir Joseph to the Doctor, or vice versa.

When the nurse announced that Mr. Huntington was ready to see them, the two men soberly entered the room. Huntington lay on the bed in his hospital shirt, his head only slightly raised and his two arms extended. With a slight motion he pointed to chairs on either side of the bed and asked his visitors to sit down. The two dealers sat stiffly in their chairs, looking at Mr. Huntington and each other and uttering everyday words of encouragement in a manner which must have been far from encouraging. Suddenly, Huntington, rather amused at the confrontation, turned to Duveen: "Sir Joseph, do I remind you of anyone?" Nonplussed, Duveen answered, "Why, no, Mr. Huntington, I don't believe so." Then Huntington turned his head toward Dr. Rosenbach. "Tell me, Doctor, do I remind *you* of anyone?" The Doctor, quite as much at a loss as Duveen, muttered that he really did not know. "Well, gentlemen," said Henry Huntington, still lying flat with his arms outstretched, "I remind myself of Jesus Christ on the cross between the two thieves." The Doctor and Sir Joseph smiled weakly.

Huntington's crucial purchase from the Holford collection was not his swan song, but thereafter he was not the main pillar of the House of Rosenbach. The Britwell sales, through which Dr. Rosenbach had been able to establish an international reputation, were tapering off, and Huntington's commissions were no longer as all-consuming—or as vital—to the Doctor as they had been. Mr. Huntington's health was deteriorating. The trimming of his sails was announced by his librarian, Bliss, who told Dr. Rosenbach that with a collection of five thousand incunables they would buy no more lots, only examples of new presses. Happily, by this time the Doctor had been able to surround himself with a host of other collectors who were ready, as the boom boomed, to buy, at least collectively, with the omniverousness of Huntington. Where Dr. Rosenbach had paid thousands in the spotlight of public auction, he now felt secure enough to pay tens of thousands. Huntington had given him the push that he needed to roll brilliantly for twenty years on his own momentum.

Many eulogies of Dr. R. were published after his death in 1952; the last eulogy will never be finished. The hammer of an auction sale, the enthusiasm of a collector, the acquisitiveness of a librarian, and the salesmanship of a dealer add to it whenever great books are bought or sold. Social changes ended the era which A. S. W. Rosenbach personified. There will be no more Huntingtons or Morgans or Folgers; there will be no more men who can build huge libraries of that kind in their own lifetimes. But there is less need for them now, for a wealth of resources has come, and continues to come, to America. In less spectacular, but no less important ways will the building of collections go on. Dr. Rosenbach believed in the importance of rare books for scholarship and in the pure joy and excitement of collecting. That belief prevails in public and private collections throughout the country. That was Dr. R's greatest sale.

Henry Moore

"I see no reason why realistic art and purely abstract art can't exist in the world side by side . . . even in one artist at the same time."

An interview by DONALD HALL

Henry Moore, generally regarded as the greatest sculptor of our time, lives with his wife and daughter in a tiny village in Hertfordshire called Perry Green, near Much Hadham. Bishop's Stortford is seven miles away, and London is only an hour by train. Behind his ancient farmhouse Moore has acquired a few acres of rolling land on which he has recently built two studios. Perched at intervals on the green field are some of his recent bronzes: a king and queen, figures upright and reclining, a draped seated woman.

When the interviewer paid his first call, the sculptor was patinating a bronze in the small old studio in front of his house. Moore, who is of medium height, solidly built, and sixty-two years old, emerged from his work wearing an apron. His face is sculptorly and massive, but not ponderous; there is a constant playfulness around the mouth; the face looks perpetually on the point of a smile.

That first afternoon, Moore showed the interviewer through his house and his studios, and they walked in the field of bronzes. Later, the interview was recorded in the drawing room of the old farmhouse, in front of a fire which burnt alternate slabs of wood and chunks of coal. On all available surfaces stood casts of maquettes and other small sculptures, and parts of Mrs. Moore's collection of primitive sculpture. Moore answered questions in kind: when he was asked to recall the events of his life, he relaxed and rubbed his hand through his hair; when the questions about his work touched his current preoccupations, his expression changed into a tense concentration while he struggled to find verbal expression for plastic ideas. As he talked, his strong hands continually molded shapes in the air.

Seated Figure (of Madonna (or Christ)
with arms extended in front
Figure in relief of arms in the
round (probably arms
attached separately)

INTERVIEWER: From what I have seen of your recent work, you seem to be mainly interested in outdoor sculpture now. Why is this?

MOORE: Well, I have always liked sculpture in the open air, and I like making sculpture which will stand outside in nature. I'm now able, for all sorts of practical reasons, to satisfy this desire, whereas in earlier days some of my sculpture had to be small in size. You can't make a small piece of sculpture stand outside in nature. It just gets lost. The open air reduces a thing in its scale. If you stood a real man on the pedestal of some of the public statues, one would find how much bigger than real life are even the things which look lifesized. They have to be.

Really, I have been concerned with outdoor sculpture nearly all my life. I had no studio, so I worked out-of-doors. It may also be that my liking for landscape and for nature has made me want to work out-of-doors, too, because I find a tremendous pleasure in actually working in the open air. To work shut inside a studio at times when the weather is good is like being in a prison for me.

INTERVIEWER: You said that life-sized sculpture outdoors needs to be a little larger than life. Are there other formal requirements for such sculpture?

MOORE: Yes. And here again I think that the habit of having open-air sculpture exhibitions may be a good thing for sculpture and sculptors. If you work in a specially lit studio, it is a temptation to push your sculpture into a position where things look better, where their less good views can be turned to the wall, and where the lighting suits them. Now in ordinary daylight—particularly English daylight, which can be very diffused and very even—only a sculpture which has a completely realized form will tell at all. Incised relief or surface scratchings won't show in dull English weather. Only your big architectural contrasts of masses—real sculptural power, real sculptural organization—will tell at all on a dull day. Therefore, if one gets used to working out-of-doors, one will be challenged into making sculpture that has some reality to it—like the reality of the nature around it.

INTERVIEWER: Do you draw as much as you used to?

MOORE: Not the kind of drawings that I used to make, which were made for their own sake. I still do drawings in notebooks, usually in an evening as I sit in this room by the fire, after a day's work in the studio. But they are not drawings which I envisage being framed afterwards or exhibited; they are either sketchbook tryouts of possible ideas for sculpture or just scribbles in which one hopes that some new idea might come.

INTERVIEWER: Why do you think you have changed?

MOORE: Perhaps because I am now doing sculptures which are bigger in actual dimensions, and so each one takes longer to do and is perhaps more continuously absorbing than the smaller pieces were. And perhaps because sculpture for me now is really the main thing and gives me nearly all that I want to do. When one is young there are lots of possibilities that one hasn't tried out; drawing is a means of finding your way about things, and a way of experiencing, more quickly than sculpture allows, certain tryouts and attempts.

INTERVIEWER: You say that sculpture is the main thing now. Hasn't it always been?

MOORE: Yes, sculpture has always been the main thing. Except that there was a time when I could be quite happy with drawing for its own sake, for months on end. That was the time of the shelter drawings and the coal-mine drawings—when for two years I was unable to do any sculpture. Afterwards I was very happy to get back to sculpture again.

INTERVIEWER: Leonardo da Vinci has a great passage in which he lists the reasons why painting is superior to sculpture. The painter makes his own shadow, among other things. Do you have any reason for thinking that sculpture is superior to drawing, or do you simply prefer it for yourself?

MOORE: I think Leonardo also said that sculpture wasn't a gentleman's occupation, that you got dirty doing it. This seemed to him a very important argument. Whereas, on the other side, Michelangelo said that sculpture could express everything. I think I know now what Michelangelo meant by that. I think he meant that since it can express so much, what it can't express you don't need to worry about, because ten lifetimes wouldn't be enough to do what it *can* do.

Another in the HORIZON interview series "THE ARTIST SPEAKS FOR HIMSELF" under the editorship of George Plimpton

---

This exploration, this attempt, this interest in three-dimensional form—in expressing oneself through solid form—this for me is the sculptor's aim. I think I am a sculptor and not a painter because I want something absolutely realized from all points of view, as *I* want to make it—something which exists, like myself or like a table or like a horse. That is the real satisfaction in making sculpture. You have really made something; you're not kidding yourself that something exists. A drawing or a painting can be read or interpreted by one person in one way or another. He may think that a certain depth is greater than another person thinks it is. Some people may think that a certain form in a drawing is meant to project *so* much. Other people may see it and think that it doesn't. In sculpture, the form actually does whatever you have intended it to do. And so you can be satisfied that you have made what you intended to make. It may be that a sculptor has that kind of nature: he wants to make a piece of reality—wants to make an actual thing.

Perhaps all I should say is that sculpture is what I want to do most, and that the less time one has left in life, the less one wants to distract or disperse one's energies into things other than sculpture.

INTERVIEWER: You originally started doing more carving than modeling. Is carving in any way a training for modeling?

MOORE: I think it's a very good disciplinary training for the young sculptor because in a stone sculpture you can't fake things so easily; you can't get away with something that doesn't exist, and you can't alter and rub out, and build up, and stick on and take off, and so on. At a certain stage in a sculptor's career I think it's a good thing to do carving. At one time I used to think that sculpture arrived at by cutting from a bigger piece down to a smaller piece—producing something by carving it down—was the best sculpture, and so my admiration was mainly for sculpture which had been produced by carving. But now I don't think it matters how a thing is produced, whether it's built up, modeled, welded, carved, constructed, or whatever. What counts really is the vision it expresses; that is, it's the quality of the mind behind it rather than the way in which it's done.

INTERVIEWER: Could you say that the center of your interest in sculpture has changed from the medium to the form?

MOORE: Yes. I think that's something like it. I think that I began with an interest in the actual physical material, and now I have become much more interested in what it turns into. At one time I would have thought it was very wrong for a piece of sculpture that had been carved in wood or stone to be cast into bronze. Now I don't think it matters at all.

INTERVIEWER: Was this a slow evolution of thought for you? Did anything you can name help to change your mind?

MOORE: No. It's only that in going on and seeing so much and such great variety in past sculpture and in nature and in organic forms and, in fact, in the whole visual world of form—which is a sculptor's world—one learns that many different ideas lead to many different results. It's no good to dogmatize on one way as being the right way or the best way. Through experience one learns that by determination—like that of a prisoner digging an escape tunnel with a broken spoon handle—you could even scratch the sculpture out with your fingernail and if it came right, it would be all right. One learns that there are more important things than the method.

INTERVIEWER: Did your original interest in method perhaps come from a necessity to attack academic sculpture?

MOORE: Yes, perhaps. When I was a student in Leeds, just before coming to London, I'd seen reproductions of Negro and Egyptian sculpture in books in the Leeds reference library, and I was very excited by these because in Yorkshire one couldn't see any sculpture other than Lord Leighton and that sort of thing. Except for examples of Gothic carvings on the local church, I knew nothing about past sculpture. I think it was perhaps my discovery of and excitement over primitive sculpture that made me more sympathetic to carving than modeling, for most primitive sculpture is carved. In those days, too, I loved stone, as I still do now. I actually love stone. A piece of stone, any piece of stone in a landscape, a big rock, anything in stone, I just love more even than I love wood. Yet I like wood, and I like clay too. Clay is wonderful stuff to punch and feel that the imprint of your fist is left in it.

INTERVIEWER: Have you ever done any wire sculpture?

MOORE: No, not in the usual way, but when you start any sculpture that's built up in plaster or modeled in clay, you make an armature first to support the clay or plaster, and this armature is a kind of sculpture made up of the center lines, the spatial skeleton, as it were, of the form you are going to make afterwards. To that extent wire sculpture is not a new invention in sculpture at all.

INTERVIEWER: Do you think it has contributed anything new to sculpture?

MOORE: Yes. In the sense that there was and still is greater interest among young sculptors in space than in solid form, and an armature has a more obvious sense of space about it, more than a single solid form has. But one eventually gets to know that the understanding of space is merely the understanding of form, that space is only the shape that form would displace in air, or the distances between two things. If you hold your hand as I am doing now, the shape those fingers would enclose if I were holding an apple would be different from the shape if I were holding a pear. If you can tell what that is, then you know what space is. That is space and form. You can't understand space without being able to understand form, and to understand form you must be able to understand space. The idea that space is something new in sculpture is only held by people who don't know what space or form is.

INTERVIEWER: How did you first arrive at your own early uses of space? I am thinking of your use of holes.

MOORE: That was the attempt to understand three-dimensional form, and to try to grasp all kinds of form, whether hollow form, solid form, form projecting from a surface or form . . . well, every possible facet of three-dimensional reality. When I first began doing stone sculpture, about 1920, the most obvious thing about stone was its solidity. I began by trying to make sculpture which should be as stony as the stone itself, but afterwards I realized that unless you had some tussle, some collaboration and yet battle with your materials, you were being nobody. The artist must impose some of himself and his ideas on the material, in a way that uses the material sympathetically but not passively. Otherwise you are only behaving like the waves. There must be a human imprint and a human idea.

I wanted to make the forms in the stone more completely realized. Instead of embedding an arm into a body—which is the way that one first begins direct carving, or rather only drawing on the surface, only making incised marks on the surface—I wanted to make forms free themselves from the matrix. I tried to divide a single piece of stone into three or four forms which had angles to each other, which thrust in different directions, in the same way that reality does. When I look at you, I see the space that is made by your head resting on your hand and the space in between; your forearm is a single mass, your head is another, your head is being supported by that forearm at present, and that's resting on the knee that juts out. All this is giving space, all this is giving action and reality to form. It's not just drawing on the surface. To understand space, I have to begin to think of actual penetrations into the stone. The understanding of three-dimensional form is never-ending, and you can separate it into experiments. By making holes through a block, you can relate the front to the back, and so on. All these things are part of one's interest in understanding three-dimensional reality.

INTERVIEWER: Your sculpture always relates to the living world. Is this on principle, or is it by inclination? Do you think that abstract art is mistaken?

MOORE: No. No, I don't. All art is abstract in one sense. Not to like abstract qualities or not to like reality is to misunderstand what sculpture and art are about. Some artists are more visual, or get more excitement from nature in front of them, and they make a work of art from that. Other people do it from their insides, a more mental approach; the actual picture-making or picture-designing can be an exercise disconnected from a relationship with the outside world.

I see no reason why realistic art and purely abstract art can't exist in the world side by side at the same time, even in one artist at the same time. One isn't right and the other wrong.

INTERVIEWER: Do you consciously try to get your mind working on a new piece? How do ideas come to you?

MOORE: Well, in various ways. One doesn't know really how any ideas come. But I can induce them by starting with looking at a box of pebbles. I have col-

TEXT CONTINUED ON PAGE 113

Henry Moore works in his studio at Much Hadham on one of his series of fallen warriors. He is making, on an armature, a plaster model that will later be used for bronze casting. In the background is a completed work, his bronze figure within a figure called Upright Exterior and Interior Form.

Perhaps! Change from bronze
to stone for UNESCO sculpture. —

Throne.

Stone same as the of building.
ie — in Roman travertine

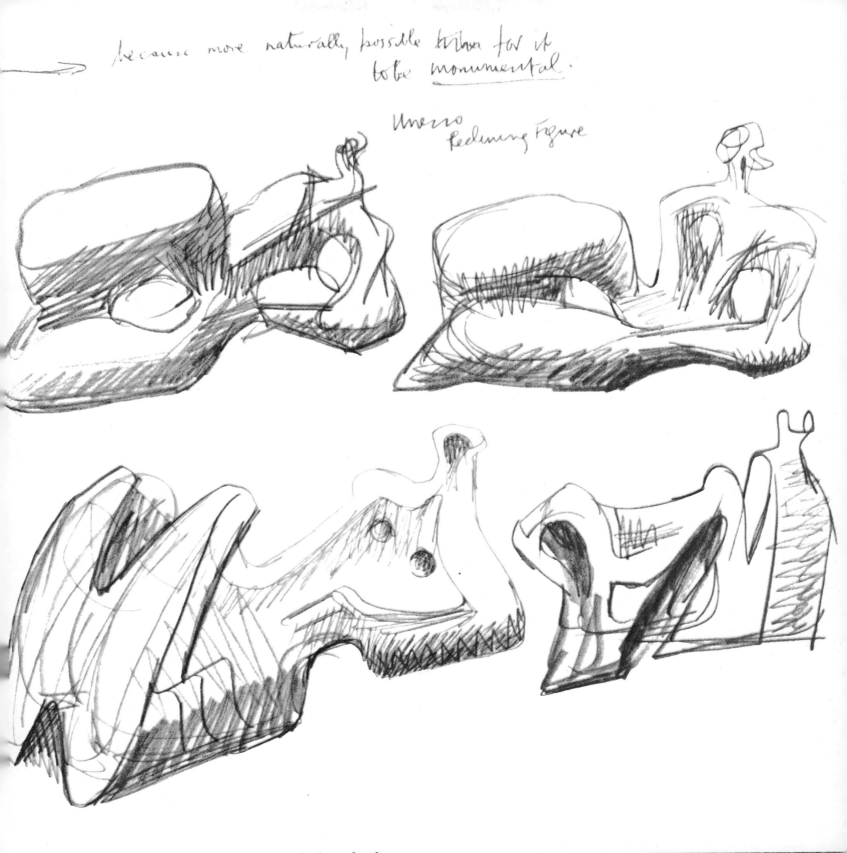

because more naturally possible titan for it to be monumental.

Verso Reclining Figure

From the beginning the reclining female figure has been a recurring theme in Moore's work. He has explored its possibilities in different ways but always with his unique sense of monumentality. These drawings and notes, which like those on page 104 are reproduced from his hand-some sketchbook Heads, Figures and Ideas recently published by the New York Graphic Society, reflect some of his preliminary thinking about his commission for the grounds of the UNESCO building in Paris. The stone figure (in photograph), finished in 1958, is six feet long. OVERLEAF: His latest reclining figures are in two pieces, one for the legs, the other for the head and body. In the eight-foot bronze finished this year, which is shown on the following pages, Moore was "trying to make a kind of mixture of the human figure and of landscape."

"The understanding of three-dimensional form is never-ending," Moore says. *He has combined holes with solids as in his reclining figure in elmwood (1935, directly below). And he has made an empty envelope which, too, is based on the figure (1954, bottom left). But he has also expressed form in a less abstract way in his moving* Warrior with Shield *(1954, below right), and in the hands (middle left) of his* King and Queen, *which appears in full on page 112.*

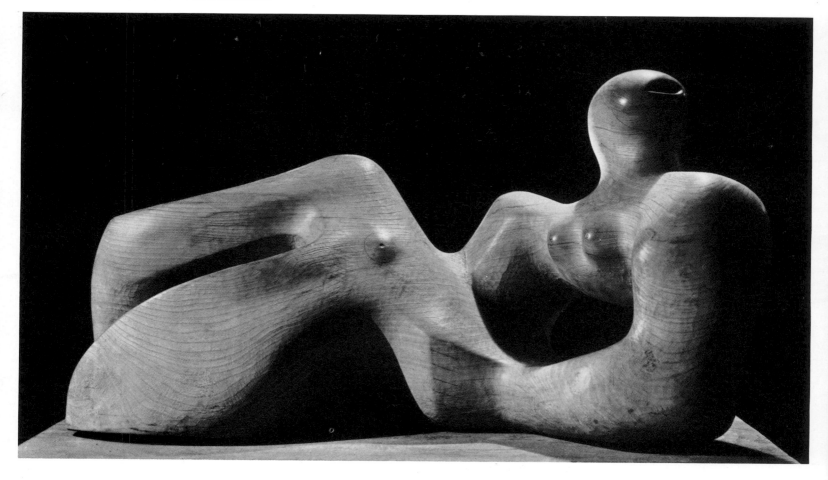

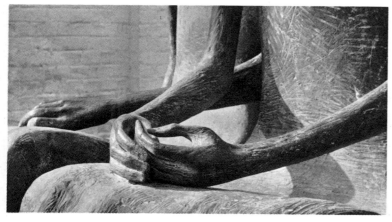

Except for the reclining figure, Moore's favorite theme has been motherhood and the family. In 1945, the year before his only child was born, Moore was commissioned to do this family group for a school in Hertfordshire. It is one of his most complex works, the result of scores of studies made over a period of five years. Of the four bronze casts made, this one stands in New York at the Museum of Modern Art in the open air, where Moore likes best to see his sculpture.

TEXT CONTINUED FROM PAGE 104

lected bits of pebbles, bits of bone, found objects, and so on, all of which help to give one an atmosphere to start working. Sometimes I may scribble some doodles, as I said, in a notebook; within my mind they may be a reclining figure, or perhaps a particular subject. Then with those pebbles, or the sketches in the notebook, I sit down and something begins. Then perhaps at a certain stage the idea crystallizes and then you know what to do, what to alter. You dislike what you've just made, and change it. At the end of a week you're sitting in that nice little easy chair with the bench in front, and there'll be probably some fifteen or so maquettes about five or six inches long, if it's a reclining figure, or that high if it's an upright. Then, either I know that a few of those are ideas I like or that I don't like any of them. If some are ones I like, then I'll do a variation on that idea, or I'll change it if I'm critical. Done in that way, the thing evolves. Always in my mind though, in making these little ideas, is the eventual sculpture which may be ten or twelve times the size of the maquette that I hold in my hand.

INTERVIEWER: Does the idea as you first conceive it have a size to go with it?

MOORE: Yes, usually. But also, one often has a size in one's mind before the idea. Now, for some reason or other—perhaps it's since I built the new studios where I've got more space—I tend to make bigger sculptures than I used to. It may also be the fact that I did the large sculpture for the UNESCO building in Paris, which was easily five or six times as big as anything I'd ever done before. That stretched my idea of size. I find now that even the smallest drawing that I make, or the smallest idea that I model in plaster in my hand, in my mind is often on a scale more than life-sized.

INTERVIEWER: I wonder if you feel that your physical circumstances hampered the ideal size of your early sculpture?

MOORE: Yes. In some of the early sculptures, I would have liked to work on a bigger size than I did, but circumstances prevented me. I had a studio in Hempstead

One of Moore's most compelling works of recent years is his King and Queen *of 1952–53. This gaunt and mysterious pair—inspired, Moore says, by reading stories of ancient royalty to his daughter—sits alone, in brooding silence, in the dramatic setting of a rocky hillside in the Scottish Highlands.*

which one had to approach up iron steps, and any stone which was over a couple of hundredweight—and that's very little for a piece of stone—became a tremendous physical problem to get in, and to get out to exhibitions. All this in the background tends to make you reduce your size a bit.

Anyhow, that thing of scale, of size, is a mixture of the two things, of physical size and mental scale. How can I explain what I mean? For example, the little sketches of horses that Leonardo made in his sketchbook were sometimes no bigger than a thumbnail, but you don't have that idea when you look at them. You think of a horse big enough to make a statue. And the same with the Michelangelo sketches. There's a mental scale independent of the actual physical scale.

INTERVIEWER: Once you have a maquette, what is the process you follow in making a sculpture from it?

MOORE: If there's one maquette which I think is more or less all right, then I'll say, "All right, this is the one I'm going to begin." I'll then decide the actual size—I shall have had in my mind the general size of something; say, if it's a reclining figure, seven feet long or six feet long or whatever —and then I'll look at the little maquette and make the adjustment for that size. I have a couple of young sculptor assistants, and between the three of us we will plan the armature. You need an armature because, with plaster sculpture, you have to build on something or you'd have a great big solid piece of plaster which is unhandleable and which takes ages to build up; so one makes an armature in wood with, perhaps, chicken wire roughly to the shape, but enlarged to scale. My assistants can do this after they've been with me for a few months or so and know the sort of methods I use. To have their help saves me a great amount of time. Once they have brought the work to within an inch or so of the measurements I intend it to be, I take it over, and it then becomes a thing that I'm working on as it would if I had brought it to that stage myself. It's more or less the same way the old masters, both painters and sculptors, worked in their time, and it's the way that's always been used from Egyptian, Greek, and medieval times. In doing large sculptures, some assistance is necessary, or you can't move or turn the work. Rodin at one time had thirty assistants.

I have two at present. They come to stay for a year or two. They're usually young

sculptors who have asked to come to work with me, and they may have already had five or six years' training in a school of art. So I can trust them to get the armature in the middle of the sculpture, and so on.

INTERVIEWER: Can you do more work modeling than carving?

MOORE: Well, it's quicker. I don't know that it's less fatiguing. Carving can be a very, very soothing, jogging-along occupation, like digging a garden. I mean, I've seen some carvers who could have done twenty hours a day at their rhythmic tapping. You can see stone carvers in masons' yards who can go on for as long as they can keep awake. It's not as hard work as people think. The difference between modeling and carving, or building up in plaster and carving, is that the modeling and building-up is a quicker thing. You can do a life-sized sculpture in half the time in plaster. And so it becomes a chance to get rid of more of one's ideas. To bring Michelangelo into the conversation again, from what one reads in his biography, he didn't want to paint. When the Pope asked him to do the Sistine Chapel, he resisted. He said he was a sculptor and really wanted to carry on with his carving. But in my opinion it's a great gain to the world that he was made to do painting. Take *The Last Judgment;* in it there are some three hundred figures, all of which are sculptural ideas, and so we've got another three hundred pieces of his sculpture, another three hundred of his ideas. In that sense it can be an advantage to use material or a medium that's quicker.

INTERVIEWER: When you feel that something is wrong with what you're doing, whether in the original stages or when you are further along, do you verbalize the problem? Do you talk to yourself in language which might sound like art criticism? Or do you simply know, as if you felt it in your hands, that something is wrong?

MOORE: In my case, I think that the verbalizing always comes after the deed. If one's dissatisfied with something, I don't think one says "What's wrong?" and "What's the way to put that right?" I think one just alters something because one is dissatisfied with it. The alteration is in a direction that one expects will make it better, but one hasn't used a kind of logical argument due to past experience or anything else. At least I don't.

INTERVIEWER: Does a sculptor find help or hindrance in the public shapes of an era? In the cars and the houses and telephone

113

poles and candy bars of our age? Does a sense of shapes originate from created objects rather than from natural objects?

MOORE: I think it's the sculptors and painters who have made the visual surrounding and not so much the architects and craftsmen. Usually the craftsmen and the architects have followed the painter and the sculptor in their form ideas. I think, for example, that Cézanne's vision and cubism, and Picasso's work, etc., produced the kind of posters we see now—rather than the other way round. I don't think that the posters will influence the young painters of today. They will ignore them. I don't think I've ever been influenced in any way by posters or by interior decoration or by the shape of the teapots you buy at Heal's. All those things are derivative. The real influence comes from the artist. Mondrian, for instance, greatly influenced the architects of his day, not the other way round. I don't think that any architects have influenced painting, not since the Renaissance.

INTERVIEWER: Yes, but different places *do* look different. The kind of thing I mean is this: Would it have done you more good to grow up among the shapes of Florence than among the shapes of Yorkshire?

MOORE: Yes, but more important than utensils, even more important than pictures or furniture or architecture, is your reaction to nature. At least it is in my case. The fact that one liked trees or stones was what was important. Otherwise, all this advertising, which is so awful, would destroy us. We would have no Cézannes, no Picassos. Wherever you are, there's nature—in the chap's body, in his girl's, in the sky, in the weather. Perhaps the industrial north, which is all soot and grime and slums, helps, because it means that you love going for walks. Within a mile of where I grew up, there were five coal mines, two chemical works, three coke ovens, and several potteries. In my youth I went walking outside the town with friends who were the sons of farmers, and I helped in the harvests. It gave me contrast, and that was the value. It's like artists not having a thing too easy.

INTERVIEWER: You work on a number of things at once. Is this on principle? Do you work on just one sculpture each day usually? Do you plan ahead which you're going to work on?

MOORE: I let the morning decide, when I wake. I don't have a plan the day before or anything like that. I've always worked on two or three things at once, but when it's

large sculpture—now that I'm able economically to do more large things—there are certain stages which take a long time and which could be tedious. So if you have another piece to work upon, after you have been doing the rather humdrum parts of a large sculpture, it is a help. But apart from that, I actually like taking time over certain pieces of sculpture, the large things, to be sure that I'm not pleased with something which was only a flash in the pan.

INTERVIEWER: Do you find that when you're working with a material like wood, which you cannot revise so easily, that you work in briefer spurts? Working only when you're very sure?

MOORE: No, because when you're carving something like wood, and it gets to the stage where you could make a mistake, an irretrievable mistake, you're not working violently. You are nibbling at the thing, and there's lots of time. It's wrong thinking for a long period that results in a mistake. If you're working slowly, there's time not to make the mistake.

INTERVIEWER: Have you ever ruined a big piece of wood?

MOORE: Well, ruining is different; a thing can always be retrieved. To bring Michelangelo's name again into our conversation, I wonder if you know what I think is one of the most moving pieces of sculpture in the world. It is supposed to be the last work Michelangelo did, the Rondanini *Pietà*, which is in Milan now, and which I saw for the first time about four years ago when it was bought by the city of Milan from a private collection. I had only seen it in reproduction before. This is a sculpture which no doubt he'd had in his studio for twenty or thirty years; it was an earlier piece of sculpture that he had altered, leaving an arm of the original sculpture still stuck. The arm had nothing whatever to do with the *Pietà*, but he left it there because if he had detached it, it would have broken off another piece that he needed. In another part you can see that although he had hardly any stone whatever to get the hand of the Madonna onto the dead Christ— there's not more than an eighth of an inch in which to do it—there's the hand, with all the feeling and with all the expression that he needs. There's always miles more material than you need. There's always more stone, more wood than what you want.

INTERVIEWER: I would like to ask you some questions about your early career. The discovery of primitive sculpture was the

greatest event in your life as a sculptor, would you say?

MOORE: Yes. But I think I'd always had the ambition, from the time I was twelve, to be a sculptor. I'd known from my school days that I liked the art lesson in school the best of all. In the grammar school I was asked to carve the school roll of honor, and I did some scroll carving on the top of it which I loved and enjoyed. For a long, long time I'd known that I wanted to be a sculptor, from the time I'd drawn the Gothic heads on Methley Church, the local fourteenth-century church.

There was a time at the College of Art in Leeds when I was a bit troubled by not liking the sculpture which the teachers there expected us to like. We were set to draw from the "antique" such things as the *Boy and Goose,* which is a late Roman copy of the Greek work, and we had to draw the *Discobolus.* I didn't have the slightest bit of interest in those sculptures, and there was a stage in the first week or two at the school when I thought, "Well, is it me that doesn't know what sculpture is? Is there something wrong with me that I don't like these pieces?"

Now I know that I was quite justified in not liking them because, besides being not very good pieces of sculpture in themselves, they'd been whitewashed every year for twenty years and had a thick coat, nearly a quarter of an inch, of whitewash on top of them, which was blurring all the sensitivity and the form. But still we were expected to draw them. Often students in the provinces don't know that they're being asked to appreciate something which in itself is no good anyhow. I think that having been brought up on bad things, having been shown bad things in the school, made one immediately recognize the good things. And it was rather the relief of discovery.

INTERVIEWER: Did the bad versions of classical sculpture for a time spoil good classical sculpture for you?

MOORE: Yes. There was a period when I tried to avoid looking at Greek—and Renaissance—sculpture of any kind; when I thought that the Greek and Renaissance were the enemy and that one had to throw all that over and start again from the beginning of primitive art. It's only in the last ten or fifteen years that I've begun to know how wonderful the Elgin Marbles are.

INTERVIEWER: Do you feel a community of aim or purpose, or whatever, with the other sculptors of this century?

MOORE: Oh, yes, with some few, of course—about four or five, perhaps. There's no doubt that the stand Brancusi took for shape for it's own sake, reducing a thing to just a simple egg, was a great help to me who was twenty years younger than he. And the cubist painters, the cubist movement, was an influence.

INTERVIEWER: Do you think that your life as a sculptor would have been different if you had been born rich?

MOORE: No. I haven't that feeling at all. I didn't have any, or not much, thwarting. Whether by luck or by circumstance, I was able to go to a school of art at twenty, when I came out of the army in the First World War, and that was quite soon enough. I am quite glad that I didn't go to a school of art at fourteen or fifteen, which was the case with lots of other students. By the time I was twenty, I was able to pick and choose from the teaching that was given to me—to decide whether I wanted to follow it or not.

And I do believe that one wants a general interest in things; one wants to know a little bit about other things besides sculpture. Some sort of general wide education is necessary even for a sculptor.

INTERVIEWER: Do the huge prices your sculptures command ever make you feel bitter over your early poverty?

MOORE: Oh, no. Of course not.

INTERVIEWER: How much do you suppose the value of some of the early pieces has gone up?

MOORE: One of the earliest big sales I made was for three hundred pounds—for a large wooden sculpture, a reclining figure, and one of the largest sculptures I'd done up to then. It allowed us to take out a mortgage on this house. I heard that the present owner of the figure was asking well over ten thousand pounds for it. But that doesn't matter. It only pleases one that someone should think it was worth so much. To us, at the time, that three hundred pounds allowed us to get this house, which we wouldn't have had otherwise. The amount that the sculpture would fetch now wouldn't mean as much to me, even if I had it, as the three hundred pounds did then.

INTERVIEWER: A great deal has changed in your life, and a great deal has changed in the life of sculpture in the modern world. Can you make any generalization about the state of the art among people now?

MOORE: I think that undoubtedly the sculpture situation is much more exciting now than ever it's been in Europe since Gothic times, or since the Renaissance. Forty years ago, in 1920, when I began being a student, I remember very clearly the position of sculpture. There is no doubt that now the appreciation of sculpture, the production of sculpture, the interest in sculpture generally, is twenty times as great. There are twenty times as many sculptors as there were then and twenty times as many galleries that will show it. There are twenty times as many people who will buy it and who will commission sculpture. This must be good for the young people. When I began, one could only hope for a few people to come along who might encourage or support one. In my time you could have counted on one hand the number of people in England who were likely to buy a piece of sculpture out of an exhibition.

I knew, from the very beginning, that if I was going to exist out of my sculpture—and not have to teach throughout my life—that I had to have my work known outside England, as well as in it. Before the war I was pleased to find that I could send work to America, and could show it in France and in other countries. One had to tap some international interest, since there wasn't enough support in this country alone.

But the fact that there were so few sculptors, I often thought, was also a good thing; then you know that everything is to be gained, that everything is to be found for oneself. There was also an excitement in fighting for one's own ideas, and fighting for sculpture generally.

I remember an article that I read by an art critic, I think in the *New Statesman*. It must have been about 1927 or 1928. The critic was also, I happened to know, a member of the British Museum staff in the Greek Department. The article was about a contemporary mixed exhibition of painting and sculpture, and when he came to the sculpture, he dismissed it. Then he had a few sentences saying that sculpture nowadays was a dead art, that it was an anachronism, and that the art of the future, if there was going to be solid art, was architecture; that otherwise sculpture was only a thing to knock your head against, and that painting was the real art. When I read this article, it made me wild. It is one of the few times that I thought of writing to the press, but I have never done it and I didn't do it. But this was the attitude then of most critics in England; sculpture was something which you could ignore, which

had no meaning any longer; it was an art of the past. And now this same person—actually I know him, but I haven't had the chance to confront him with it—must know what a difference there is between what he thought and what has happened. He thought it was safe in those days to say that sculpture was a dead art.

INTERVIEWER: Lately, as you have said, you have been able to have young sculptors as assistants. You probably have contact with a good many others. What kind of advice can you give the young sculptor?

MOORE: It would depend on what stage the young sculptor had arrived at, and what his difficulties might be. I think that older people can help younger people if they are in a quandary, if they are worried, or if they are muddled up. For instance, in 1925, after I came back from my traveling scholarship in Italy, I just didn't know what to do. I had looked at the old masters for a longer period than I intended, and when I came back, having looked for five months and not done much work of my own, I was terribly het-up and worried. For five months I had been looking at things with my cap in hand, instead of doing work, which would have been the healthy state for a young person of my age. Also it was just when I was at a most inquiring and experimental part of my own work. For six months, when I came back, I think I had the most miserable time of my life. I was trying to digest and sort out the conflict between the Renaissance and my ambitions born of looking at primitive sculpture.

If I had asked for advice at that time, the advice that I hope I would have been given is what I found out for myself eventually: to start working again and not to bother whether the work is good or bad, but just to work. I think lots of young people get into states about their work—if they are poets, about their poetry; musicians about their music. The way of getting out of these depressions is to work them out, to actually produce, to make yourself *do* something with it. If you can force yourself into working when you don't feel like it, that brings a mood for working naturally afterwards. This is the main advice that I'd give to all young sculptors. Keep on working. The thing solves itself in the end.

Poet Donald Hall, who spent the past year in England, interviewed Archibald MacLeish for the January, 1960, issue of HORIZON.

115

THE CRITIC'S VIEW

THEATER
This Blessed Plot, This Shakespeare in the Park

The New York theater in the past several years has become a three-part activity —Broadway, off-Broadway, and Shakespeare in Central Park. The third is my present subject, and I find it rather tricky. Joseph Papp, founder, producer, and often director of the New York Shakespeare Festival, easily falls into the mold of those plucky heroes who supplied our grandfathers with their inspirational reading. He can't be beat because he won't be beat, and as a consequence, he has provided the citizens of New York with productions of twelve plays over a period of seven years—and charged not one penny for admission. With no money of his own and no close relationship to money, he has created a meeting place for "a dispossessed audience and dispossessed actors." Meanwhile, he has held a full-time job in television to support his family.

Papp is no philanthropist; he is an idealist and an optimist, but these are different matters. The Shakespeare Festival is an utterly surprising gift to the people of New York; it is also, for the present, a bold and ingenious solution to a personal quest, worked out by a tough young man of powerful ego and daring imagination.

Papp's idealism consists in believing that every citizen needs and is entitled to a theater—just as he needs and is entitled to schools, libraries, and museums —and that actors deserve an alternative to the "talent-destroying" gamble of

Broadway. His optimism consists in believing that others will share his vision of a theater run for beauty and wisdom, not for money.

Thus began a shoestring operation so audacious as to seem almost ludicrous. "Shoestring" is, however, not the word for it because that implies a desperate scramble for solvency, and Papp has never had the least intention of becoming solvent. He *expects* to be supported and, curiously, his strength is that he has always made that clear: "What is basically needed is the conviction that the arts are vital to our lives. Methods of financing will follow."

Papp's method of financing is to announce each season what plays he proposes to stage and how much they will cost (seasonal budgets have risen from a few hundred dollars in 1955 to $100,000 for 1960) and then to start rehearsals. He has steady nerves and is capable of opening a play when he has no funds beyond the first night. Some seasons have been chopped short, but in the main, Papp has made good his announcements. Money has been forthcoming: it has come chiefly from foundations, but a steady small stream has come from the audience. Public funds still elude the Festival, but various city departments have given invaluably of materials, equipment, and services. When the 1960 season ended, the city was committed to building a $250,000 permanent stage for the Festival, and Tyrone Guthrie was

scheduled to direct *Hamlet* for the first offering in the spring of 1961.

In addition to bringing Shakespeare to the people, Papp brings a number of good young actors before a very large audience. Besides George C. Scott and Colleen Dewhurst, this number has included Jerry Stiller and his wife, Anne Meara, both excellent Shakespearean comics; Jack Cannon, who has played Touchstone and Tyrrel, among other roles; Peggy Bennion, John McLiam, Robert Blackburn, and Robert Geiringer. Papp's theater is not yet so solid an institution as the Public Library, but it is nevertheless an institution.

Now obviously there is a trick to this. You cannot simply throw yourself from a rooftop, crying "I will fly, I will fly," and expect anyone to express more than momentary interest. You must show some aptitude for flying. The first thing always said of the New York Shakespeare Festival is that it is free, but the more important fact is that it is good. The public is said not to appreciate anything it gets for nothing, but night after night, summer after summer, the long line forms at the gate to the Festival grounds and waits as long as three hours for admission. The present theater holds 2,500; it plays to full capacity six nights a week for approximately ten weeks, and on many nights the fences are lined with spectators who arrived too late to get in. People come in the tens of thousands, not because the seats are free—every bench in Central Park is that—but because they are aroused and instructed by the play. And because they come to be fed, the money comes to nourish them. That quarter-mile queue, stretched out between the lake and the playing fields in the twilight, is a breadline, and Papp is of a background that teaches the moral force of breadlines.

Excellence has been the trick from the beginning. Back when the Festival was still the Workshop, and *As You Like It* was being performed without sets or salaries, Meyer Levin wrote of "the pace of the direction" and "the precise note of stylization" of this "unadulterated Shakespeare." And in the seasons since then, first at the East River Park amphitheater, later touring the boroughs with a portable stage, now based in Central Park with winter seasons at the Heckscher Theater on upper Fifth Avenue, the productions have elicited similar comment. The critics do not indulge the Festival (they applaud the idea, but judge the product), and notes of sharp criticism have been directed at this characterization or that interpretation. But the Festival has enjoyed what is known as a "good press," and the phrases of appreciation fall into a pattern: the plays are vivid, they move fast, they are exciting and credible, they are clear, and they seem pertinent. Levin astutely compared the Workshop to the New York City Ballet—all the classic knowledge is kept, but accumulated "tradition" is stripped away and a freshness gets into the material.

Papp finds himself, he says, at odds with the subjective muddiness of the contemporary realistic theater and seeks a style that rests initially on the words of the play, not on the acting. What an actor does should follow necessarily from what he says; he makes his bearing congruous with his lines and does not seek readings of the text that support a "characterization." From this stem several corollaries for Shakespeare: the manner to be sought is heroic—in gesture and clarity, bigger than life—but based on a respect for the characters as real people (even in the Festival's Forest of Arden, the people were extraordinarily real); the action should be *on* the lines, not between them; scenes should move at such a pace that one actually pushes another off the stage; and speech must not only be clear but sufficiently rapid so that the long line of Shakespeare's ideas does not falter.

The ideal is a poetic theater, based on a conviction that the matter in hand is important and relevant to the audience. None of this is easy, and I would not wish to give the impression that it is perfectly achieved. But the program gives a method of approach; it offers the actors—often inexperienced ones—a rational basis for building their parts, and it produces a particular Festival quality. Shakespeare is in vogue at the moment, and on various stages we are offered a variety of brilliant, painstaking productions. But often they tend to be elegant museum pieces or are "translated" into our times and concerns. I know of no company that is as successful as the New York Shakespeare Festival at finding the eternally contemporary in Shakespeare and presenting it, without strain, in its Elizabethan idiom. You get the eeriest feeling, in the Park sometimes, that Shakespeare is alive and among us.

A good way to find out how strong an idea has become is to try to stop it. Robert Moses tried to stop free Shakespeare early in 1959 (he was then New York Parks Commissioner), announcing that he would not renew the Festival's license unless tickets were sold at $1 and $2 with 10 per cent of the gross going to the Parks Department for sundry expenses, including repair of eroded grass. Papp refused.

Mr. Moses, a man of varied talents, has never been a good judge of public opinion and periodically finds himself playing the role of villain to a large and aroused audience. No one has explained why he turned on the Festival after earlier expressions of approval, but it is obvious that he did not foresee a formidable uprising on behalf of Shakespeare. Nonetheless, the uprising occurred and Mr. Papp found a vocal throng of supporters; Mr. Moses received the obloquy of both press and populace for his part in the affair.

Papp took Moses into court and was supported by Justice James B. McNally of the Appellate Division, who instructed the Commissioner to reconsider his "arbitrary, capricious and unreasonable demands." Moses, now feeling hemmed in, tossed the Festival to another city department, saying in effect, "you can have your free Shakespeare if the Board of Estimate will give me $20,000 for my erosion." Two private citizens, Edward Bernays and Mrs. Florence Anspecher, offered the money. By June 24, the Festival was back in Central Park, but with time left for only one play, *Julius Caesar*. It was acclaimed on all sides.

Last summer, Papp opened the season by directing *Henry V*, Alan Schneider followed with *Measure for Measure*, and Gerald Freedman completed the schedule with *The Taming of the Shrew*. Looking at the first two productions together, one can see what constitutes the Festival style. Young Harry's conquest of King Charles's realm and his daughter's hand was, of course, a happy choice for the Park. The Festival's "wooden O" rang with the clash of personalities and the implied collision of armies. At the same time, Papp's emphasis made it perfectly clear that the subject of the play is less the struggle between France and England (about which no one now desperately cares) than the determination of the fledgling and notorious Hal to show himself a king of mettle and the legitimate leader of his land. Youth has come into power—the king and his handsome brothers—and though it is disposed to honor and heed the experienced guardians of the state (as shown most sweetly in a fine rendering of the scene with Sir Thomas Erpingham, that valorous old knight), it will not tolerate ambiguity of authority. Thus the moment is one of great uneasiness until Henry demonstrates that he is strong enough to grasp his realm with grace and honor. This is a drama that never loses relevance, and Papp found in James Ray an actor able to express the quiet, intelligent force that Shakespeare implied below the surface of Harry's neophyte swagger and youthful heroics.

The staging of *Henry V* was gallant with light and rich cloth and the flash of armor. But every embellishment functioned—every torch lit a dark corner, every brazier warmed a cold soldier, every banner was there to lift the hearts of a ragged band of commandos. And certainly no one moved but to a purpose—this *Henry V* plunged ahead as though caught in a flood, and indeed it is a story of men caught in the flood of events.

By comparison, *Measure for Measure* vacillated, cast about, and lost its momentum. The comparison, I know, is unfair to Schneider, for not only was he directing his first play in the Park—he is the first director other than Stuart Vaughan or Papp to work there—but he was engaged with a play that can only with the greatest difficulty be made credible to modern audiences. (The Festival, though, scored one of its early successes with *Two Gentlemen of Verona*, a play you would have thought no one could reanimate today.) There were good things about this *Measure for Measure:* in particular, Philip Bosco created a convincing Angelo, making of him a shocking but somehow touching man, and the play pulled itself together for a resolute and meaningful conclusion. But Schneider let his worries show. They showed in the heavy earnestness with which the cast spoke its lines—arguing, as it were, with the audience instead of one another (the actors often were players I knew to be excellent from earlier productions). And it showed in a kind of fussiness of staging (though this was the most handsome of all the Festival productions I have seen) that seemed to be trying to assist Shakespeare. A procession of nuns was beautiful, and beautifully killed the action; a chess game was introduced, served no purpose, and was sheepishly put away; the Duke stepped on a high platform to deliver a soliloquy (why should a man get up on a box to talk to himself?); Angelo sanded his papers so industriously during the first encounter with Isabella that the scene looked more like a lesson in penmanship than a plea

for mercy. Busyness is the death of action.

And the characters strained. Lucio is really at the heart of *Measure for Measure;* if you make him credible, you have gone a long way toward making the play credible. Frederic Warriner was encouraged to turn him into a kind of lewd puppet, winking, smacking his lips, playing glissandi with his voice, hopping about like a beset blue jay. Lucio is, in fact, almost a comic Iago, a man of wit and malice, a good fellow and rotten. Of all the sins in the play, his calumny alone is unforgivable. True, he is extravagant, but no more so than the Dauphin in *Henry V,* with his tennis racket and his apostrophe to his horse. Thomas Aldredge made sense of that fantastic; he showed us a youth of precocious promise, spoiled by his elders and bored by them, and overcome by Aubrey Beardsley. Every campus sports a few—and about half grow up to their talents.

I could go on—the comics of *Henry V* were off the streets, the comics of *Measure for Measure* were out of some theory of acting—but I don't want to carry the comparison further than the point requires. The point is that Shakespeare rewards only those who trust him. It is no good saying "they will never take that scene if we play it straight," because it is certain that "they" will not take it if you try to apologize for it. The Festival's quality rests on the fact that it has always assumed that Shakespeare is good enough; that he created people, not characters; that values and behavior change, but motive and impulse do not. It has drawn its pictures with the largest, simplest, fastest strokes it could devise, working outdoors in the Park as though on a mural, with strong design, bright color, and sure motion.

This year, Papp gave up his job in television. He has instituted a subscription program whereby patrons contributing $7.50 are invited to previews of the Festival productions. The anticipated 10,000 subscribers will not only add to the annual budget but will be an active support to the Festival.

So Papp's ingenious scheme for a re-

warding life in the theater for himself and his actors, and a theater for the joy of all comers, approaches reality; but its inventor is still not satisfied. For one thing, he wants to be granted a continuing appropriation by New York State's Department of Education. He thinks he has proved that he is an educator, and he does not fear government control: "There can be no guarantee of freedom in the theater or any place else. . . . It is a condition that must be constantly fought for."

He does not plan to restrict himself indefinitely to Shakespeare ("I'm no crazy Bardophile," he once said) and is even now looking speculatively at Shaw's *Saint Joan.* And he does not intend to confine himself forever to Central Park. It is a superb site; it will be better still with the permanent installations. But for Papp it has the drawback that, in the center of Manhattan, it attracts too high a proportion of the regular theater public. He recalls nostalgically evenings on the East River when men and women cried out in protest or approval as the unknown drama unfolded, when children ran down to the rim of the stage to menace or support the players. This still happens in Central Park, but not often enough to suit the producer. He wants to tour the neighborhoods where at present the only drama is delinquency. This was his early plan, but it broke down in 1957 because it took eighteen hours to set up and dismantle the equipment and because the mobile stage was falling to pieces. With the Park base now reasonably secure, Papp is scheming for a better truck stage on which he can take Shakespeare to people who do not know whether Macbeth will live to enjoy his throne or what fate awaits Juliet.

The New York Shakespeare Festival is an astonishing success, but it does not seem to astonish its founder. He said some time ago: "You start with the philosophy that theater is important to people's lives. If you don't believe this, then you might as well give up. Of course it's true. A spirit handed down for 2,000 years and more can't be ignored."

——ROBERT HATCH

BOOKS
Only Yesterday: The Third Reich

When I was at school and college, history was what happened long ago. This was one of several reasons why it was so dull and difficult. We learned all the names and careers of the Plantagenet monarchs. We were enjoined to remember that they were French by origin and sympathy. But we learned little or nothing about Queen Victoria and her dynasty, still reigning, and we never realized that they were German by origin and sympathy. Certainly, although I was at school both during and after a great world war, my teachers never dreamed of discussing that war in history classes. The facts were not fully known. Much vital information about the causes and progress of World War I was still hidden in secret archives. Many of its great strategic maneuvers were known or understood only by specialists. (I remember being perfectly astounded in the 1930's when I met one of the German officials who sent Lenin and his group across Germany in a sealed train to St. Petersburg, in order to relieve the pressure on Germany's eastern front.) Many of the issues involved, both moral and political, were obscured by national loyalties or confused by elaborate chains of causation.

Not so today. History is now. Or at least—in the words of Frederick Lewis Allen, who brought the immediate American past into focus for his own generation—history is "only yesterday." Of the recent events through which many of us have lived, and which have shaped the lives of everyone on the planet, there are many comprehensive historical studies; and more appear every year. Mr. Schlesinger's story of the era of Roosevelt is moving on from volume to

volume, always lively, always intelligent, always clear. Two of the great men of our century, Churchill and De Gaulle, have published their memoirs in the shape of historical surveys, meditations, and reassessments. Adolf Hitler, for understandable reasons, left no history of his own times. (If he had, it might well have been called by the title devised by one of his brain trust, *The Myth of the Twentieth Century*.) Still, the diaries and memoirs of a number of his associates, underlings, and opponents, living and dead, have recently been issued. Reconstructions of various crucial events in Hitler's career have been made by intelligence officers, military analysts, and diplomatic observers. What is far more important, a vast treasure of German archives was captured after Hitler's ruin and is now in the possession of American, British, and Canadian authorities. Using these multifarious and often conflicting materials, William L. Shirer has produced an admirable study of one of the greatest events since the death of Napoleon, *The Rise and Fall of the Third Reich*.

This is one of the finest histories of its type, and it is unlikely to be superseded for many years. Mr. Shirer's style is sometimes flat-footed and seldom rises to real eloquence. But, because he is an experienced reporter, it is always as clear as glass, and often vivid. His book is lit up by many moving personal reminiscences. Five years, he says, the work took him. They were five years well spent.

History, says Gibbon, is "little more than the register of the crimes, follies, and misfortunes of mankind." Some tender hearts will shrink from reading the story of the crimes and follies and mis-

fortunes which were brought into being by Adolf Hitler and which were to afflict so many people for so long. The very voice of Hitler is still in our ears—that powerful, unflinching, yet flexible voice, half the shout of command and half the howl of mania; and, with it, following upon it like the roar of a flood after the crack of a dam, wave upon wave upon wave of the massed voices of Hitler's Germans. His very face is still in our mind's eye: the face that so many men studied, not in admiration, but in the hope of solving its enigma; the features that once looked commonplace and almost vulgar, and which grew to obsess all but the strongest minds—those who, like Thomas Mann, could see it as the mask of a malicious demon or, like Churchill, as the brutal front of a bloodthirsty guttersnipe. The ruins of his war have been largely rebuilt. The frontiers he changed have been redrawn. The loot he and his henchmen stole has been recovered, or buried and forgotten. The corpses whose death he caused are burned or interred. What profit or pleasure can there be, many will ask, in reading his story, however clearly and compellingly it is told?

There are horrors in *The Rise and Fall of the Third Reich*, but it is not wholly or even mainly a horror story. It is intellectually engrossing. Sometimes it has the deep interest of events which are familiar but are only half-understood. World politics are beyond most of us. Few can grasp the problems of economics. Hardly a single soldier comprehends the war he is fighting. Of the tens of millions of people who saw, and felt in their flesh, the rise and fall of the Third Reich, very few could detach their emotions sufficiently and command enough information to realize, except in the vaguest outlines, what was transforming their world. Many of the greatest events went by so rapidly that, like a jet plane, they were gone before they could be identified. It is scarcely possible to live through such a series of events, to have them fixed indelibly in the memory, without being gratified and somehow spiritually enlarged by learning later the essence of history as Ranke defined it, "how it really happened."

Take one crucial instance. We remember Pearl Harbor. On the "date that will live in infamy" (as F.D.R. with his fine classical eloquence described it), the Japanese initiated hostilities against the United States. On December 8, Congress formally declared war upon Japan. Within the next few days, like a furious epidemic, war spread from continent to continent. Before Christmas, 1941, the United States, after almost a generation of peace, was compelled to fight not only the Japanese aggressors but the Germans and the Italians and their European allies and satellites. But why? Very few of those who remember Pearl Harbor can recall accurately how and why —after we became involved in the Pacific conflict that had been forced upon us—we were also sucked into the most perilous type of war, a war on two fronts far removed. Mr. Shirer's twenty-fifth chapter makes this problem clear.

Hitler, with his right hand in the Russian wolf's mouth, and trying with his left hand to strangle Britain and the European resistance, had not wished the United States to enter his war. On March 5, 1941, he stated one of his basic strategic aims: to set Japan against Britain in the Far East and to "keep the United States out of the war." The only wise strategy for him would have been to treat Japan in its struggle with America as America treated Britain in its struggle with Germany: with benevolent and beneficent neutrality, this side of war. But his power of calculation was leaving him. He could never see far beyond Europe, and his fantastic successes of 1940 had begun to drive him mad.

His attack on Russia was a gamble which might have succeeded. He lost it, in December, 1941, to General Mud, General Snow, and General Zhukov. Rather than trying to hold fast in Europe with the hope of overthrowing, if not the Russian armies, at least (as in 1917) the unpopular Russian government, and then negotiating a European settlement, he made a further gamble and ensured his downfall. He declared war on the United States also. Mr. Shirer traces several of his motives for this action, all powerful (for such a man) and all unreasonable: (1) he admired the Japanese initiative and wished to "strike the first blow" himself; (2) he personally hated Roosevelt, as he made clear in his Reichstag speech proclaiming hostilities; (3) he despised the United States as a nation, telling his friends that same winter that the country was "half Judaized and half Negrified"; and (4) he forgot, or idiotically underestimated, the enormous potential of America, not only in industry but in manpower. Once again, neither for the first time nor for the last, Adolf Hitler was making history; and it was unmaking him.

Sometimes—this is one of the best things about Mr. Shirer's book—it tells us secrets which, although they affected the lives of myriads of men, were subtly and securely hidden for long years and which are still largely unknown to the world. The most important is the secret which was disbelieved: that throughout Hitler's years of power there was a long-standing and eminently important movement of opposition to him inside Germany. Rumors of this opposition were heard by the Allies during the war, but they were usually discounted. Since the Allies had called for unconditional surrender, it seemed pointless to think about a party that might try to negotiate something different. Or to put this another way, many of Hitler's opponents were eager to overthrow him so as to keep Germany powerful and the German army in being, and most people outside the Reich thought this an evil purpose. Some members of the opposition were idealists who shrank from

the factual necessities of power politics: they talked with angelic nobility but would not kill Hitler and disrupt his power machine. Even those who tried, failed, because of something eccentric and almost inexplicable. Hitler himself called it his "fate" or even "Providence." It baffles Mr. Shirer, and it will baffle many future historians. But perhaps it is the fundamental stupidity that infects highly organized men when they try to destroy a complex social pattern. Even at the climax of the one conspiracy which was almost fully effective—when a bomb planted by an officer exploded under Hitler's map table, wounded the Fuehrer himself, and killed many of his staff; when a military rebellion headed by generals was taking shape as far west as Paris; and when the dictator was, for three hours, cut off from communications with his empire—the vital hours were somehow wasted. The Germans are always brisk and ruthless in taking action against "inferiors"—a term which includes all non-Germans. When they think of opposing a tyrannous superior of their own stock, they are paralyzed.

Sometimes, though, history of this kind induces an intenser experience, which is a deeper kind of discovery, a more inward knowledge: the amazement of fantasy. For decades before the rise of Hitler we were told, by loud and convincing voices, that war was impossible in a world which was principally civilized. For generations we heard that German culture was lofty, that German morals were strong. For a century we believed that slavery had been finally abolished and that torture by legal authority was a fading nightmare of the past. Then all these idealistic illusions were struck into splinters. The old torture chamber in Nuremberg, with its gross but effective equipment, was still being shown to tourists as a romantic relic while the physicians and policemen of the Third Reich were preparing instruments of far finer scientific efficiency and marking down their future victims. Slavery, for some time, had been half-acknowledged in Russia as "a corrective institution." The Germans under Hitler refined it into an important element of industry. As for German morals and German culture, they existed only in somber exile. Inside Germany there were many who greeted this transformation with rapture: a hope fulfilled, a dream come true. Outside Germany, it was a nightmare, which nevertheless had teeth and claws, breathed fire and poison, ate people alive. When we read today about all that barbarism, we are bewildered. It would be happier for us all if we could believe it had never happened. It did. As a result, we know more, for good and for evil, about the human spirit. A sur-

vivor of one of the Communist slave camps wrote a grim description of the Russian occupation of Poland and of life in prison and called it *The Dark Side of the Moon*. He should have remembered the torture-religions of the past and the slave politics of the present and called it *The Dark Side of the Mind*. C. G. Jung foresaw this years ago and wrote that, while primitive man is afraid of savage animals, earthquakes, floods, and volcanoes, "the gigantic catastrophes that threaten us are not elemental happenings of a physical or biological kind, but psychic epidemics."

Hitler, and those whom he infected, were not only mad themselves, they were symptoms of a widespread disease. In the physical domain, we know the answer to many problems of health (although we do not necessarily use them). In the realm of the spirit, intoxicants and impurities are freely peddled; intellectual viruses spread from country to country and increase by interbreeding and mutation. In *The Rise and Fall of the Third Reich*, we see not only the maladies of the past but, dimly and forebodingly, a prognosis of the future.

——GILBERT HIGHET

MOVIES
War and Peace in Two Foreign Films

On the evening in June when I saw *Hiroshima, Mon Amour*, the newsreel preceding the feature included a sequence showing President Eisenhower being clamorously greeted in Seoul; he responded with wreathed smiles and the gesture—cordially shaking his hands above his head—that declares, "I'm all right, Jack." In the midst of the hearty din, the commentator observed parenthetically, in a solemn voice, that the behavior of the Koreans was in sharp contrast to that of the unsociable and mercurial Japanese, who had altered the position of their latchstring from out to in. Later on, we saw the President golfing in friendly Hawaii, and this time we were reminded that his reception *there* had been in sharp contrast to the inhospitality that had confronted him in Okinawa. The newsreel ended with a fine, stirring, uncontroversial scene of detachments from Queen Elizabeth's dressy regiments going through their paces in a tattoo at Madison Square Garden.

The kilted chaps in this last treat re-

called to me my first visit to Scotland in 1949, and I was still thinking pleasurably of lochs and glens and the skirling of bagpipes when the dolorous-gay, Oriental-Occidental, ancient-modern, tentative-conclusive background music of *Hiroshima, Mon Amour* introduced the film. This enigma is constructed of as many laminae as baklava, that Near Eastern confection made of layers and layers of paper-fine pastry, deliciously agglutinated with honey, in which are embedded fragments of nuts. Like baklava, *Hiroshima* is filling; unlike baklava, it did not satisfy me. It is too puzzling; one is not certain what one has eaten and does not know, therefore, what condition one's palate is in. This is not to say that the sensation and the experience have not been interesting, indeed engrossing, but we tend to want to know whether we have liked or have disliked what has happened to us. It will only be after revisiting the movie over a period of years that I shall be able to see it as a whole, and perhaps I shall

never be able to.

The plot presents no complexities: in Hiroshima, more than a decade after its catastrophe—rebuilt and westernized with neon lights and Hiltonic hotels—a French actress, who is in the city to make a documentary film on peace, meets and falls in love with a Japanese architect. Both are married and, though at the end of a handful of halcyon and poignant days their passion has not subsided, their reason reigns, and the woman, having finished her work, returns to France. On this factual level, we are persuaded that they will never meet again, that they are responsible and mature enough to know that the encounter can have no sequel. On one of the more obvious symbolic levels, we are offered the thesis that all men are brothers and that, though East is East and West is West, the twain can meet if the representative of each is intelligent and has meditated the conflict of ideologies and the transgressions of countries against one another and has concluded that, under the aspect of eternity, both are meaningless. But on a somewhat different plane, we have the feeling that the lovers are doomed, like Dante's Paolo and Francesca, to drift in each other's arms until the end of time, punished with satiety, though the one dwells physically in Japan and the other in France.

Through the most remarkable manipulation of time-shift I have ever seen on the screen (flash backs within flash backs, flash backs antedating flash backs, and flash backs subsequent to others, never at any time suspending the continuity of the narrative, a remembrance of things past told in the urgent present tense), it is revealed to us that the actress as a young girl in Nevers during the war had been in love with a German soldier, had been consequently despised, shorn of her hair, and driven to insanity by her humiliation and by grief over her enemy lover's death. Her disgraced parents had kept her in a cellar, where her screams could not be heard, for two years of nightmare. At length, when her hair began to grow out and the pain of her bereavement to recede, she began to rise like a phoenix from the Gehenna of her own making. Yet the question presents itself: *Was* it of her own making any more than Hiroshima's was of its? She was too young to have had the selflessness to repudiate her first love for the nebulous love of country; her ramparts had been no better defended than Hiroshima's.

In the very opening scenes of the picture, the Japanese reiterates gently but adamantly that the woman could not possibly imagine the hell and holocaust after the bombing of Hiroshima, and she as firmly insists that she could and did, that she *knew*. It is not until much later on, when the flash backs begin, that we realize her knowledge derived from her own interior torture. At first we believe simply that she had an uncommonly profound reaction to the newsreels in the summer of 1945. Excerpts of these and shots of molten rock and tangles of steel and photographs of hideous human deformities, exhibited in the museum erected as a memorial to the dead and

devastated (visited by sightseers who descend from buses labeled "Atomic Tour"), constitute so grave an admonition that perhaps they should be shown compulsorily in schools throughout the world. We are all guilty, we have all collaborated with our enemy, but our enemy is our own creation. If *Hiroshima, Mon Amour* is to be interpreted as an allegory, then I take the architect to be the new Japan, rising above its dismay and its perdition, committing the act of forgiveness by the act of rebuilding. This reflection, when I had left the theater, made Eisenhower's abortive trip to the Orient, reported by Pathé, the more pathetic.

The juxtaposition of newsreels, short subjects, and feature films is often curious indeed. Soon after I saw *Hiroshima*, I saw the Soviet importation *The Cranes Are Flying*, which is also concerned with the horrors of World War II. The preliminaries this time dwelt at considerable length on General MacArthur receiving Japan's highest military honor in peacetime, an accolade never before awarded an enemy commander. It was too kaleidoscopic: the once acclaimed ex-General Eisenhower now booed, the once booed ex-General MacArthur now acclaimed; I gave up trying to figure out where I was at. After the mortal facts and before the immortal fiction, I watched a fancy perpetrated by UPA and starring nearsighted Mr. Magoo in the role of a baby sitter who mistakes the dog for the baby, putting the *Homo sapiens* out for the night and tucking the *Canis familiaris* into a comfy bed with a nippled bottle of warm cooking sherry. I wondered what symptoms of capitalistic depravity would be read into this mild joke if it ran in the USSR on the same bill with *The Cranes Are Flying*. Would we be scored for pressing so venerable a man into service as a nursemaid or for letting a dog, in our wasteful way, lead the life of Reilly?

But I doubt that the creators of this extraordinary movie would have objected to Magoo; they might have been perplexed and unamused but not censorious. The propagandists have not stuck a single oar into *Cranes*; it is in

the great Russian literary tradition of Dostoevsky and Tolstoy, taking as its subject the whole classless landscape of the human heart with its ravines of despair and pinnacles of nobility and by-paths of foolishness and delight. The story, as in *Hiroshima*, is essentially a simple pastoral tragedy: tricked and confused by the dislocations of war, orphaned by an air raid, the heroine marries a wastrel (draft-exempt through chicanery) while her fiancé is at the front fighting a bitter war that eventually kills him. Veronica's guilt is compounded by the fact that Boris, the soldier, and Mark, the slacker, are cousins, and she, living in the heart of the family, must bear the unspoken contempt of Boris's sister, the disappointment of his forebearing father, the pity of his grandmother. Through dreadful months of the war in Moscow and in Siberia, she cannot relinquish the hope that Boris is only missing, and it is not until the war is over and the troops return that she can accept the incontrovertible certainty of his death. And having accepted, she now can do nothing—if she is to remain alive—but forgive herself. Thus, at the end, we see her threading her way through the throngs at the railway station, giving away the flowers she had brought for Boris—to reunited lovers, to bearded old men, thrusting wilting daisies into the paws of wartime babies. Her smile bespeaks her renascence.

Both of these movies are in black and white, and the chiaroscuro in both seems to me infinitely more effective than if they had been made in color. In both, the long shots (the girl in Nevers riding her bicycle along a country lane, distantly observed by her German lover; Veronica and Boris running along the embankment of the Neva) give intricate impressions of distances within and distances beyond. And in the close-ups, even at moments of greatest pathos, neither causes the eye to water. If the purpose of art is to teach and delight, then both are works of art, though neither, thank heaven, is schoolish, and both are a little more bitter than sweet.
——JEAN STAFFORD

122

ADVERTISING
The Glass That Wasn't There

Just about a year ago, Earl W. Kintner, chairman of the Federal Trade Commission, ordered a handful of his employees to glue their eyes to the nearest television set and come running the moment the odor of dead fish emanated from one or more commercials. As a consequence, Mr. Kintner and his agency have gone from one triumph to another, and enough information has leaked out about the procedures of our better advertising agencies to alter the whole aspect of television. I myself have taken to using my Little Master Remote Control in reverse, eliminating the programs and fixing my attention solely on the commercials, and I think I am a happier man for it. This, however, may not be very much of a tribute to Mr. Kintner.

The best-publicized complaint was the one issued against Libbey-Owens-Ford and its agency. To recapitulate briefly, the sponsor had generated an urge to advise the public that L·O·F glass was a good deal easier to see through than non-L·O·F, or Brand X, glass and requested that the agency bring the matter to the attention of the viewing audience. This was accomplished by taking moving pictures through ordinary glass (labeled Brand X) and through no glass at all (labeled Libbey-Owens-Ford). In still another commercial, the unsuitable characteristics of Brand X were delicately emphasized by smearing it with Vaseline before taking the pictures. The company and its agency have been asked to cease and desist and are pretty much put out about the whole thing.

In a sense they were victimized by their attempts to cope with a little-known fact about motion pictures: left to itself, nothing ever looks quite right on film, which is a highly unnatural way of presenting information and must be firmly disciplined. If, for example, you wish to convey some intimation of the sights and sounds of Paris, the worst mistake you can make is to take a camera crew abroad. Everything shot in Paris will look like Akron, Ohio. The proper procedure is to paint up a few flats, lean them against the wall of a sound stage in Culver City, California, and start the film rolling. Such are the perversities of silver nitrate emulsions.

The FTC, of course, is well aware of these facts. They have no objection at all to the beer advertiser who wishes to show the luxuriant foam on his product and accomplishes this by spraying the surface of the beer with shaving lather. All the FTC asks is that if the commercial shows a competing beer, this must be sprayed with the same lather. In other words, if L·O·F had shot *both* pictures through thin air, it would have been all right with the FTC, although it would not have been much of a commercial.

Speaking of shaving cream, the commission also took umbrage at a Palmolive Rapid Shave commercial which showed someone—it may have been Yogi Berra—shaving a swatch of sandpaper. The Commission righteously pointed out that it wasn't sandpaper at all but merely some Plexiglass with sand on it. The way it stands now, as I understand it, Palmolive maintains its cream *will* shave sandpaper, and the FTC says it *won't*, and two more glorious irrelevancies would be hard to come by. The question of whether it will shave Yogi Berra has been lost in the shuffle.

Mr. Kintner has also attempted to lower his administrative boom on tooth-paste advertising—Colgate's and Pepso-dent's, to be precise. Here my sympathy lies entirely with the advertisers. Tooth paste *is* advertising—advertising with color and artificial flavor added. There is nothing the best tooth paste in the world can do for your teeth that isn't done quite as well by a handful of twigs and some water from the nearest (running) stream. At least, that's what my dentist tells me. He has refused, so far, to be stampeded by the American Dental Association and their recent love affair with Crest. My dentist once had a patient whose teeth itched, so it is obvious he is a man of wide experience. Anyway, it is my contention that tooth-paste advertisers, and soap advertisers in general, should be encouraged to make any claim that comes to mind; otherwise, Procter & Gamble might stop spending the $100,000,000 or so it devotes each year to advertising, and the entire American economy might thereupon crumble. It just might.

As might have been expected, the advertising industry is not happy about this new assiduity on the part of the FTC. Its wounds are not economic, since the structure of the industry is such that it ordinarily turns a decent profit even on its mistakes. The blow is to self-esteem. The most grievous wound suffered by ad men in recent years resulted from the fact that in both the Republican and Democratic national conventions last summer, and in the campaign which has followed, the phrase "Madison Avenue" has been used as an epithet denoting contempt. The Republicans, too, you understand. The industry, whatever its achievements in other fields, has been a lamentable failure in selling itself, and Mr. Kintner is not being any help.

—STEPHEN WHITE

THE NEWEST INVASION OF EUROPE

CONTINUED FROM PAGE 16

distinguished by the Rhine, which gives it a superb river frontage, and by the Königsallee, a stately boulevard lined with the smarter shops and the more progressive businesses and institutions. At its northern end, the Allee approaches the Rheinfront in the Hofgarten, an area of greenery and ornamental water, and it is here that the two new towers stand: the Mannesmann block (pages 12–13) just back from the Rheinfront, and the Phoenix-Rheinrohr building (page 14) farther inland, on the other side of the axis of the Hofgarten.

Both buildings were commissioned by giant manufacturers of tubular-steel products, so both have tubular-steel frames and are clad in curtain-wall glazing. But there the resemblance ends. Mannesmann, designed by Paul Schneider-Esleben, was guaranteed international acceptance from the start, not only because it is one of the most elegant small skyscrapers in the world, and one of the most beautifully detailed throughout (the profiles of the glazing bars on the exterior are of the greatest subtlety and originality), but also because it is another of the Sons of Seagram.

Phoenix-Rheinrohr, on the other hand, designed by Hentrich and Petschnigg (the German Skidmore, Owings and Merrill, give or take a partner) is an original; no other skyscraper in the world has the same plan-form or massing. The vertical core of centrally placed elevators and services was placed in a thin slab of building no wider than itself, but flanked on either side by slightly thinner, smaller, and lower slabs, with narrow access corridors between one slab and the next. The result looks something like a double-decker sandwich—with the slices cut from different-sized loaves—stood on end.

This is a purely European design, a step away from the original made-in-America concept, a step toward whatever kind of tall building eventually fulfills specifically European needs. Even so, Phoenix-Rheinrohr does not tackle the whole European problem because neither it nor Mannesmann has the usual difficulties of site and aspect. The townscape of the Königsallee and the Rheinfront tends toward large islanded blocks, and the two towers follow the trend, with only marginal worries about their siting. Mannesmann had to be polite to an older office block, designed by the great Peter Behrens for the same firm, which it immediately flanks; Phoenix-Rheinrohr, it now appears, will overshadow the site of the new Düsseldorf *Schauspielhaus*, but this poses no great problems—the winning design for the theater, by Bernhard Pfau, uses the flat side of the towers as a foil for its own low, cylindrical forms.

In London, however, problems of siting have been at the top of the argument; and there is now a massive bibliography of articles, reports, lectures, symposia, and memoranda on the subject, not to mention protest marches, letters to *The*

Times, and ill-informed obiter dicta by archbishops and peers of the realm. After the war the official planners of the London County Council, taking into account the improvement in fire precautions and the change in taste, gave its blessing to the planners of tall buildings with certain provisos. One is that, short or tall, a building is still governed by the plot-ratio for its zone; that is, there is an absolute limit on the amount of floor space it may contain—in practice, the higher, the thinner. Also, the constituted authority retains pretty nearly absolute control over the siting of tall buildings: certain areas are effectively taboo for skyscrapers; and, in the areas where they are permitted, the way in which legislation is administered and the way in which the consultative services of bodies like the Royal Fine Art Commission are employed have tended to impose a minimum distance of about a quarter-mile between one block and the next.

In part, the reasons for this are practical and unarguable —it prevents local overloading of services and traffic facilities, and on the positive side the quarter-mile rule tends to force new tall buildings out of successful areas into languishing ones where there is less competition for sky space. The new building is seen as an aid to the regeneration of such run-down districts.

But there has been an aesthetic motive too. One of the chief fears has been that skyscrapers would intrude, out of scale and out of style, into views of the kind of eighteenth-century survival that Londoners and visitors alike admire— in the way that Castrol House (page 14) now looms over all southward views of the compactly Georgian Dorset Square. Determined that big towers should not gang up and smother areas like this, planners, preservationists, and townscape enthusiasts united to insist that tall blocks should stand well apart and be related to large-scale visual features—much as the tower in Eastbourne Terrace (also page 14) makes a skymark at the head of the Long Water in Kensington Gardens.

But as soon as this policy began to be carried out, there was a revulsion against it, particularly among Londoners who enjoy wide views over the city, as from the heights of Hampstead or the front windows of Buckingham Palace. The prospect of a London skyline regularly accented with thinly spread towers according to the quarter-mile rule was seen to be as dull as the London skyline evenly built up to the 100-foot ceiling, and there is a growing feeling that the rules should now be waived in such a way as to encourage sporadic close-clustering of taller towers (say thirty-five stories) rather than the twenty-story average they run to at present. But this is still in the debate stage, and it will be at least four years before one can see if it is going to happen.

Curiously enough, the actual appearance of the buildings has never been an issue in the argument, probably because there has been little—apart from the much-hated Shell building nearing completion on the South Bank—to argue about. All the London towers of note are either Sons of Seagram or descendants of the Ministry of Education building in Rio (though forthcoming developments like the Elephant and Castle may put an end to this phase). Most are extremely competent; none—in honesty—is a work of even near-genius. Castrol House, by Gollins, Melvin and Ward (the English Skidmore, Owings, etc.), with Sir Hugh Casson and Neville Conder, is the best of the Sons of Seagram, but not comparable with Mannesmann in Düsseldorf in ultimate quality and refinement, though it is well sited and its nighttime appearance has been carefully thought out (rare, this, in Europe). Eastbourne Terrace is, for the moment, everybody's beau ideal of a London skyscraper development. It has two towers—one tall, one middling—placed in a properly designed setting of lower blocks; the whole operation is socially admirable since it effected the rescue of the whole of one side of a bomb-ruined street and brought smart, executive-type employers (such as advertising agencies) into a run-down district. It lacks visual sparkle, being soberly faced in traditional materials (a preference of the architect, Cecil Elsom), but it carries great architectural conviction, and convinces even non-Londoners like Gillo Dorfles, the Milanese critic.

Conceivably, Dorfles was relieved to meet a skyscraper which he could praise for its simplicity—it would be difficult to do the same for most of those in Milan. Like Düsseldorf, Milan is smart, bustling, progressive; but the smart bustle here rests on a foundation of continuous civic history that goes back at least to Roman times, and the continuity can be felt. It shows in many things, but for me, the symbol of that continuity is the archbishopric ("the chair of Saint Ambrose," second only to the papacy in Italy) and the mad Gothic cathedral that enshrines the tradition of Ambrosian episcopacy.

It is precisely this cathedral that bedevils the Milanese skyscraper argument. Until recently, the cathedral's crocketed pinnacles shared the skyline with nothing but a few thin, square campaniles that did not compete with it in any way. Nor, really, did the first two or three skyscrapers; they stood a little way off, in obviously commercial places like the Viale Vittor Pisani, and were square and thin like the bell towers. The argument hung fire for some years because everyone was waiting for the two really big, controversial skyscrapers to go up, and it was not until 1959 that these could be confronted.

Completed, they represent the extreme poles of the city's character. The Pirelli building (page 15) is Milan at its smartest and most technological, least heedful of the past. Designed by a group headed by Gio Ponti, the personification of *gusto milanese*, and Pier Luigi Nervi, past master of Italian concrete engineering, it is technically brilliant and need not yield place even to Phoenix-Rheinrohr. But it is feared that its siting prejudices any future replanning of the area around the Central Station, and its whole character shows a cavalier indifference to the traditions of Milanese townscape. It is the most consciously *modern* building in Europe.

The opposite pole is represented by the Torre Velasca (page 15), in a more built-up, more history-laden area, much closer to the cathedral, and designed by the partnership BBPR. The final R stands for Ernesto Rogers, a lover of London's—and Milan's—traditional townscape, a man of conscience who feels on his shoulders the full weight of history and everything untranslatable that comes with the word *cultura*. The Torre Velasca was designed with the cathedral always in mind; the design was many years maturing, and over those years, while the bulk form remained much the same, the details and the profile against the sky became ever more Gothic.

The result gravely disquiets most European modernists, not least because it is far from being a feeble compromise with craven historical revivalism. With great moral stamina in the face of hostile criticism, Rogers hammered out an architecture that he believed to be right in this situation, and with it he made a very positive architectural statement that puts other Milanese skyscrapers on trial. I don't think that it finds them all guilty, but it raises some very awkward questions about an architect's responsibilities to what Rogers calls the *ambiente preesistente*, the town that was there before.

No European architect is free, in his own mind, to proceed as if history and civic traditions did not exist. He can consciously acquiesce, he can consciously modify, he can consciously defy them. Once it enters his mind that the building he is designing is in any way a skyscraper, he knows that he is introducing a foreign concept into his native scene; and he can never design it in the frame of mind in which he designs a house, a church, a bridge, or even a tall building of a different form, such as a television tower or a big slab of flats like Le Corbusier's Unité d'Habitation at Marseilles.

The European skyscraper is a stranger in the land, and it will still be a stranger even after it outnumbers other types of urban buildings, as it probably will in great commercial centers. Its acceptance depends, and will still depend long after the contrary has been proved in experience, on its symbolic power as a sign of a new and better order of life. Architects will, for a long time, approach the thing itself with enthusiasm, its consequences with suspicion. These opposing pulls may paralyze creative thinking, or they may stimulate it; and the evidence of Velasca, Eastbourne Terrace, Phoenix-Rheinrohr, and a half-dozen others is that it may yet stimulate European architects to make a significant and original contribution to the architecture of tall buildings. They may also have a lesson to teach American architects, now that skyscrapers like the Flatiron building are attaining the Williamsburg status of monuments of national culture.

As assistant executive editor of London's Architectural Review, *Reyner Banham is a constant observer of the architectural scene in England, on the Continent, and in America.*

THE INNOCENT AMUSEMENTS OF JEAN ANOUILH

CONTINUED FROM PAGE 55

"pink" plays that end well; "brilliant" plays that please; "jarring" plays that displease. But he seldom speaks of his own work, and then always semi-ironically. Writing for the stage, he claims, is only "my innocent way of amusing myself while entertaining others. . . . I do not have posterity in mind—those children still in their early years on whose opinion we set such store, I really wonder why—nor the respect of my contemporaries. . . . I write only for my entertainment—heaven, good fortune, the times, and work, too, have allowed me to offer myself the only real luxury: freedom."

Anouilh likes to say that he turns out plays as others turn out chairs, a remark designed to emphasize his distaste for the "metaphysical" aspirations of some contemporary playwrights. This does not mean that he is not deeply, though indirectly, involved in each of his plays or that they do not reflect his own, sometimes passing, moods or points of view. It is significant that as he moves along in life, the central figures in his plays tend to move along with him. In the first plays the hero was often a young man in love, like Frantz or Orpheus. But now that Anouilh is well into middle age, his heroes are older men: poor aging General Saint-Pé in *The Waltz of the Toreadors*, a character who is called merely "the General" in *Cry of the Peacock* and *The Fighting Cock*, and the apparently successful old windbag in *Ornifle* (not yet seen in America)—a modern Don Juan who is threatened not by the irate statue of the Commendatore but by a less picturesque heart attack.

"When I listen to Chekhov," Anouilh has said, "I become a small boy again, and I hear an old, hopeless and tender melody which could have been mine if heaven had so decided." But heaven decided otherwise. It was this Chekhov mood he had in mind, he tells us, when he started to write *Cry of the Peacock,* but "at the fourth rejoinder" in the opening dialogue, "an old and not at all Slavic demon appeared, forcing me to be ironic, and I let him have his way." The ironic demon in Anouilh lives side by side with another very tender, almost sentimental demon, "the only thing that always saves men from themselves, in the long run—a little love." The peculiar and instantly recognizable atmosphere of Anouilh's theater is due to the strange games these two demons play with the characters and situations he invents. He has a strong sense of the disproportion between a human being's feelings and his place in the world; between his capacity to suffer through others and the basic selfishness of the "man-insect"; between the inner drive for some form of dignity and the pettiness of its outward manifestations. In Anouilh's eyes, man is a "social being only accidentally"; he is essentially, as André Breton once said, "a definitive dreamer." To Calderón's "life is a dream," Anouilh

answers "a dream is life." He sees the people around him as baffled and tricked by an existence that makes no allowance for what is best in them—their dreams.

Man, as Anouilh sees him, is "an inconsolable and gay animal." From that point of view, there is very little that separates the unsuccessful entertainer, eking out his existence in mean cafés, from the legendary hero. "We can wound each other, betray each other, massacre each other in the name of more or less noble pretexts, dilate ourselves with imagined grandeur: we are funny. Nothing else. All of us, whoever we may be, our heroes included. The boring philosophers of despair who, periodically and a little naïvely, discover the horror of the human predicament and want to prevent us from enjoying the theater had better resign themselves to the fact: we are funny. And, in the long run, this is even more atrocious than their frightful descriptions of our futility."

We are funny; we are gay and inconsolable; selfish and brutal as insects; perpetual dreamers capable, sometimes, of a little love—all of us baffled and betrayed by an ironic fate that hands us a "part" to play. Here theater and life coincide: it is the playwright who distributes the parts in a play; it is he, too, who decides how they will be played and how it will all end for the participants. In a sense, therefore, the characters are innocent. There are really no villains in Anouilh's theater. Even when one of the characters in *The Rehearsal*, sardonically named Hero, basely and deliberately seduces a young girl, he is pitiful rather than villainous—the victim of the same crime that he perpetrates: the destruction of an inner *élan* toward love and purity. He has been cast in his role and he must play it to the end.

A great deal has been written about Anouilh's *Antigone* in contrast with Sophocles's. But little mention has been made of the basic assumption in the play, characteristic of Anouilh and certainly closer to the Greek than to the Christian vision of life: fate has prepared Antigone's role and she must play it out, no matter how or why. The Greek Antigone can perhaps rationalize it as the will of the gods. Anouilh's Antigone has no recourse but to accept the part and play it: she cannot escape. All of Anouilh's plots are based on the game that an ironic fate—benevolent in the *pièces roses,* malevolent in the *pièces noires*—plays with the characters. And plots they are, in both senses of the word.

For this game, Anouilh likes to draw on characters or situations that have already been dramatically conventionalized, "stage" characters and situations. This preference is easy enough to recognize when his characters are historical—Joan of Arc, Thomas à Becket—or legendary, like Antigone and Creon, Medea and Jason, Orpheus and Eurydice. But it is just as true of characters that seem to have been invented by him. Ornifle, for example, is a modern Don Juan, and

lowing the Queen's State Coach. The golden coach itself appears in the second panel, from which a detail is shown in color below. The third panel is a parade of military units, among whom the most easily distinguishable are the pike-carrying Beefeaters in their ruffs and tall hats. Then, in the fourth panel, a crisp and characteristically English note of dissent sounds forth amid the fanfares. Here Topolski has pyramided the faces of some of the most vigorous critics of England's so-called Establishment—the members of what might, in fact, be called the "Anti-Establishment." In the detail below, from top to bottom, may be recognized Julian Huxley, Bertrand Russell (in profile), portraitist Augustus John, the late Aneurin Bevan, and the young playwright John Osborne.

The four panels at the top of these pages continue Topolski's fantasia on the coronation procession. In the upper left-hand corner of the first one are the ubiquitous photographers—floating, as it were, behind their cameras. In the center foreground, men of the St. John Ambulance Brigade are carrying away the fallen (fainting casualties). Behind them and to the right, workmen are hastily cleaning up the litter as the massed bands of the Foot Guards sweep down from the center rear. At the right of this panel, members of the upper classes are decorously watching the procession. The second panel depicts, on the left half, the Queen Mother's procession and, on the right half, the processions of Princes and Princesses of the Blood Royal, preceded by their escorts.

The thoroughly regal figure of Queen Salote of Tonga, a British protectorate in the Pacific, dominates the third panel (which is also reproduced in color below). Scorning the vast umbrella behind her, she rode on —drenched but smiling—through the rain.

In the lower left corner, sheltered by another umbrella, is Winston Churchill in the robes and bonnet of a Knight of the Garter. The fourth panel shows, at lower left, part of the crowd that slept in the streets the night before and, in the foreground, peers

and peeresses in ermine and coronets. They are preceded by the Duke of Norfolk, who opened the proceedings. The crowd closes in again at the extreme right. It includes a famous old London vagabond, Mr. Feathers, and—at the very bottom—Topolski himself.

The ancient rites within

The second part of Topolski's mural is composed around the coronation ceremony in Westminster Abbey. It consists of only six panels, somewhat shorter than the others since they are mounted between windows. Portions of the first two are shown in detail below. The massive head at the left is that of the Dean of Westminster leading the procession. In the middle are the Heralds Pursuivant and behind them the officers of the Orders of Knighthood. In the right foreground are the brooding faces of some of the

Commonwealth prime ministers, ending with the monumental, stubborn-jawed visage of Winston Churchill. Behind him is the Keeper of the Jewel House. The third panel above includes, in the immediate foreground, the Sultan of Zanzibar and Crown Prince Aki-

hito of Japan. The central figure with the rich fall of ermine is Prince Philip (detail in color on page 129). The fourth panel depicts peers carrying the Regalia, most noticeably the Sword of State. And then, in the fifth panel, comes the climax to all this accumu-

lated magnificence, as the newly crowned Queen (see detail in color, overleaf) moves in stately procession down the aisle, followed by her Maids of Honor. The great pageant is brought to a close in the final panel, where the last members wait their turn to fall in.

Crowned and consecrated, the Queen proceeds through Westminster Abbey supported by the Bishop of Durham and of Bath and Wells